THE FUTURE OF
FOREIGN LANGUAGE
EDUCATION AT
COMMUNITY COLLEGES

EDITED BY
DIANE U. EISENBERG

This AACC publication was prepared with funding from
the National Endowment for the Humanities.

American Association of Community Colleges
National Center for Higher Education
One Dupont Circle, N.W., Suite 410
Washington, D.C. 20036-1176
(202) 728-0200

© Copyrighted 1992
Printed in the United States
ISBN 0-87117-248-8

TABLE OF CONTENTS

Part I

PREFACE

DAVID R. PIERCE

O N FEBRUARY 9–10, 1992, THE AMERICAN ASSOCIATION OF COMMU-
nity Colleges (AACC) convened a roundtable meeting of
education leaders with expertise and experience in foreign
language education and community college teaching and
administration. The roundtable participants met to address key issues
related to foreign language instruction and to formulate a foreign
language education policy statement for AACC setting forth specific
recommendations for foreign language education at community colleges.

This publication is the result of their efforts. It includes the policy
statement, which originated with the roundtable recommendations
and emerged following an elaborate review and refinement process in
which all community colleges were invited to participate. In addition,
the publication includes five essays on selected foreign language education topics which were prepared as background papers for the
roundtable.

The Association's new foreign language education policy statement
poses a most timely and relevant challenge for our nation's two year
colleges—a challenge that is consistent with our over-arching mission,
that of *building community*. When we improve foreign language
education opportunities for our students we enhance their capacities
to function in and understand an increasingly interdependent world;
in effect, we contribute to *building community* in the broadest sense
of the term.

The American Association of Community Colleges deeply appreci-
ates the support it received from the National Endowment for the

*David R. Pierce is President and Chief Executive Officer of the American
Association of Community Colleges.*

Humanities (NEH) which enabled it to provide leadership to its colleges in setting directions for the improvement of foreign language education on their campuses. We are also indebted to Judy Jeffrey Howard, NEH Program Officer, for her commitment to and belief in the nation's community colleges, and to Diane U. Eisenberg for conducting the roundtable and preparing this resulting publication.

Judy Jeffrey Howard at the AACC Foreign Language Education Roundtable, Washington, D.C.

Diane U. Eisenberg, Co-director, AACC Foreign Language Education Policy Statement Project, at the 1992 AACC convention.

Part II

FOREWORD

JAMES HERBERT

I T IS A PLEASURE TO CONGRATULATE DAVID PIERCE, THE AACC BOARD of Directors, Diane Eisenberg, and the project staff on this timely initiative to foster the study of foreign languages and cultures in two-year colleges.

The roundtable background papers are an important resource to the field, highlighting some of the exciting language programs already in place at colleges across the country. Effective models include strong classroom programs, including content-based and technology-enhanced instruction, languages across-the-curriculum projects, study abroad and exchange programs that include occupational as well as transfer students, and programs for life-long learners in an array of commonly taught as well as newly emphasized languages. The roundtable papers incorporate information on recent advances in foreign language pedagogy and assessment as well as on the key role that community colleges can play in coordinating the necessary sequencing of language study from elementary school through college.

As the National Endowment for the Humanities continues its Special Opportunity in Foreign Language Education, it is gratifying that AACC is taking a leadership role in encouraging two-year colleges to strengthen programs of study in foreign languages and cultures. For information on NEH support for foreign language projects, please contact the Public Affairs office at (202) 786-0443 or the Division of Education Programs at (202) 786-0380.

James Herbert is Director of the Division of Education Programs at the National Endowment for the Humanities.

"As a nation in a global economy, our economic competitiveness will partially depend on our citizenry's ability to understand the language and culture of the countries with which we do business. Foreign languages are becoming increasingly common within the borders of our own country. Our ability to live and work with people whose native language is not English and/or whose culture patterns are different from our own is fast becoming a focal point for our society."

> Beverly Simone
> President Madison Area Technical College, WI;
> Chair, AACC Board of Directors

"A great irony of the United States' marvelous multicultural society is that a large majority of its citizenry remains culturally isolated. A major key to opening doors to other cultures, to richer insight into one's own culture, and to important linkages among all cultures is second language acquisition. Community colleges are uniquely situated to take the lead in transforming U.S. citizens into intercultural communicators. The need is urgent."

> Stephen K. Mittlestet
> President
> Richland College, TX

Part III

AACC Foreign Language Education Policy Statement

The Study of Foreign Languages at Community Colleges

A. Foreign Language Education: A National Priority

Foreign language education has become a national priority. Leaders from many sectors of American society—federal, state, and local governments, the business and corporate sector, labor and education—insist that foreign language instruction must be an essential part of the education of citizens for today's and tomorrow's increasingly interdependent world. Elected officials, economists, cultural leaders, corporate executives and educators at all levels are concerned about an America whose citizens cannot understand, converse or do business in a multi-linguistic world—a world in which global cooperation and peace depend not only on sound policy, but on effective communication. These leaders recognize that the ability to read, write, speak and comprehend the language of other peoples, as well as the ability to understand both one's own heritage and the culture of other peoples, has the power to transform rivalries and competition into partnerships and cooperation.

For a host of compelling reasons, which resound in the many national reports published on this subject, our country's education sector is being called upon to respond by preparing students to understand and communicate in today's rapidly changing world. This policy statement aims to assist community college educators to meet

This statement was adopted and approved by the AACC Board of Directors on July 1, 1992.

the considerable challenge of making foreign language education a national priority.

Meeting the Challenge Through Language Proficiency and Cultural Understanding

The approach that educators take to meeting the challenge must be two-fold: language instruction must encompass both language proficiency and cultural understanding. By achieving both language proficiency and cultural understanding learners gain insight into the cultures of other peoples, understand better their own language heritage and culture, and can expand their career opportunities in ways that otherwise would not be accessible. To pursue one without the other leaves learners unprepared for today's opportunities and challenges, as well as ill-equipped to perceive themselves as one part of the world's varied cultures.

To be proficient in a language requires that one know more than words and grammar; one must know how to read, write, speak, and comprehend at effective levels. Cultural understanding requires that students study the history, literature, philosophy and arts, as well as the modes and rituals of everyday life of other peoples. These two approaches go hand-in-hand.

For these reasons, effective foreign language instruction must be inextricably linked to the goals of a general education and particularly to the study of the humanities. The study of foreign languages within the context of a general education and the humanities enables students to reflect on and understand concepts of self and society through different eyes.

Equal attention must also be given to language proficiency. Despite keen current interest at all educational levels in global education, educators often fail to incorporate the study of foreign languages themselves into these programs. Students cannot fully appreciate the people and cultures across or within borders without some competency in the languages they speak. Students cannot understand their cultural ancestors without knowing about the languages they spoke. Students and their future employers cannot hope to thrive in a world where competitors hold the linguistic keys to success.

Therefore, the nation's educational institutions must meet the challenge of providing effective and responsive foreign language instruction—instruction that encompasses both language proficiency and cultural understanding.

B. Foreign Language Education: A Critical Responsibility for Community Colleges

The nation's community colleges must make profound commitments now to this new national priority. Community colleges, more than any other sector of higher education, are serving those segments of our population most in need of foreign language education. Among these are:

- the increasing number of students who are taking the first two years of the baccalaureate degree at community colleges before transferring to four year institutions;
- students who need foreign language proficiency for technical, occupational and professional careers; and
- adult part-time learners who seek to improve their foreign language abilities.

It must be emphasized that the study of other languages is no longer the sole province of transfer students and foreign language majors; it is an indispensable tool of modern life and should be a part of every community college student's education. Community colleges have been historically touted for their flexibility, their pioneering talents, and their ability to respond to the needs of non-traditional learners. These institutions must now mobilize these capacities to make foreign language acquisition a priority for all their students.

It should be noted that many innovative and academically rigorous language education programs are already in place at the nation's two year colleges and available for replication. Among these are:

- foreign language certificate programs
- intensive immersion programs on campus, in the community and through study abroad
- literature-based foreign language programs
- foreign language across-the-curriculum programs
- media-enhanced foreign language programs
- programs of instruction in less commonly taught languages
- programs in American native languages and cultural studies
- programs that infuse ancient languages, such as Latin and Greek, into cultural heritage studies

With vision and planning, language study can become a significant component of the community college curriculum. Unlike colleagues at four-year colleges, where upper-level literature courses, graduate programs, and critical study are driven by the specialized interests of faculty members, community college faculty have the capacity to combine basic foreign language instruction with cultural education in customized courses, special programs, and the full spectrum of credit/non-credit continuing education and community service programs. Community college faculty know their student constituencies and can shape language courses and programs to meet both particular and general needs.

The Need for Collaboration With Other Educational Sectors

No matter how well positioned and able community colleges may be to improve foreign language education, they cannot do so in a vacuum. Learning a language is a prodigious task. A meaningful level of foreign language proficiency cannot be achieved in a single course or even in a year of study. For example, one year of Japanese will not produce competent conversationalists or readers capable of mastering technical journal articles. Three semesters of French at the college level will only begin to prepare students to read significant works of literature written in French.

Community colleges must assume a leadership role in working with elementary and secondary school systems and four-year colleges and universities to develop meaningful and long-term articulation with their foreign language programs. If language study is not encouraged and accepted as an integral part of the curriculum from grade school through the university level, the current failure of students to master second languages will continue.

Call to Action

The nation's community colleges must advance the study of foreign languages in a direction that will serve the educational needs of a diverse citizenry in the twenty-first century. Existing traditional models alone are not sufficient to serve the community college's non-traditional students, nor will they serve the increasing numbers of transfer students. A commitment on the part of college leaders, the availability of adequate resources, campus-wide discussion and the setting of curricular and instructional priorities are precursors to the development of effective foreign language education in the community colleges of the nation. The recommendations that follow are offered as guidelines for community colleges seeking to accomplish these goals.

C. Recommendations to Community College Leaders

Making Foreign Language Education a Priority

In order to create a campus climate in which foreign language education can flourish, commitment and support toward implementing the following recommendations must be declared and made public by the faculty and the highest policy and administrative bodies— trustees, presidents, academic deans, and other administrators.

Recommendation 1. The *study* of foreign languages should be highly recommended for all students, including those with academic goals other than a degree program.

Recommendation 2. Foreign language *proficiency* should be a requirement for those degree programs to which it is appropriate. To this end it is recommended that such degree-seeking students be required to demonstrate a minimum of "survival-level" proficiency in the four skill areas of speaking, listening, reading and writing*.

Recommendation 3. Foreign language programs should be administered and taught by qualified foreign language educators.

Recommendation 4. Each community college, with leadership from its faculty, should develop a comprehensive plan that identifies the purpose and methods of language instruction appropriate to the particular needs of that college's diverse constituency.

Strengthening Foreign Language Education

Foreign language education must be strengthened to engage students beyond the most basic level of language acquisition. Students

---

*"Survival level" proficiency is the minimum level at which students have the functional ability to ask and answer questions, to speak and write simply about familiar situations in a present time frame, and to negotiate a simple interpersonal transaction.

must also understand and appreciate the cultural context in which other languages are spoken, read and written.

Recommendation 5. Educational policy concerning language education and the place of other languages in the two-year college curriculum should be framed within the context of an overall policy on the humanities in the liberal or general education program of study; foreign language education should not be considered in isolation, but rather as an integral part of the overall college curriculum.

Recommendation 6. Community colleges should create teaching and learning environments conducive to successful foreign language education by being sensitive to class size, faculty teaching loads, the attainment of appropriate training for all faculty, and an appropriate balance between full-time and part-time faculty.

Recommendation 7. Foreign language instruction should broaden, and not compete with, required humanities courses. Historical, literary, philosophical, cultural and other works in the arts and humanities should be infused into all language courses and programs.

Recommendation 8. Community colleges should examine ways in which new technologies, used in conjunction with qualified foreign language educators, can enhance language instruction.

Recommendation 9. In addition to basic and intermediate level foreign language courses, community colleges should expand the scope of language study to include a broad range of diverse offerings such as languages across-the-curriculum programs; immersion experiences and enhanced study abroad programs; paired humanities/foreign language courses; cross-cultural institutes, workshops, and conferences.

Recommendation 10. Community colleges should enrich their foreign language programs by reaching out to their local community of native speakers, including those in professions, business and government agencies.

Strengthening Faculty Development

To encourage and assist language teachers in enhancing their scholarship, refining their teaching skills, and continuing in the profession, the following recommendations are offered:

Recommendation 11. Faculty development resources and external funds should be made available to help language faculty to:
- further their knowledge and proficiency;
- improve their teaching skills;

- design new programs;
- develop competency in oral proficiency assessment; and
- learn new applications of technology.

Recommendation 12. Full-time faculty, and where possible, part-time faculty, should be encouraged, supported, and rewarded for active involvement in scholarship and the activities of professional organizations which focus on the quality and improvement of language instruction.

Improving Articulation

Continuity in language learning is essential to effective foreign language education; it must take place throughout the educational process. Community colleges, serving as the link between high schools and four-year institutions, are well-positioned to address problems that now impede articulation.

Recommendation 13. Community colleges should take a leadership role in their service areas to build an alliance of elementary, secondary, two- and four-year colleges, graduate schools, and other appropriate local bodies to address the full spectrum of articulation and continuity issues in language education.

Recommendation 14. Community colleges should initiate communication with four-year colleges and graduate schools in their service areas regarding teacher education, so that these institutions can come to understand the instructional needs of the diverse two-year student body and develop better prepared teachers to meet those needs.

These recommendations, developed to make foreign language education a priority at community colleges nationwide, should be circulated widely to boards of trustees, college administrators, legislative officials, and college faculty, as well as to public and private press and other media.

D. BACKGROUND

The American Association of Community Colleges (AACC) received funding from the National Endowment for the Humanities (NEH), to:

- address key issues related to foreign language instruction;
- make specific recommendations for improving foreign language education at community colleges.

To accomplish these purposes, AACC convened a two day foreign language education roundtable on February 9-10, 1992, co-chaired by David R. Pierce, President, AACC, and Diane U. Eisenberg, project co-director. Twenty-one participants, selected for their expertise and experience in language education and community college teaching and administration participated in the roundtable. They responded to a set of five specially-prepared background papers on language education topics and developed a set of recommendations for community colleges. These recommendations were then submitted for review and refinement by community college leaders nationwide, prior to adoption by the AACC Board of Directors.

The recommendations presented herein are addressed to community college leaders—presidents, governing boards, faculty, administrators, and curriculum committees. Responsibility for placing the importance of foreign language study before the college community and mobilizing activities in its support belongs to each community college president.

Part IV

BACKGROUND PAPERS

D A V I D A. B E R R Y

Foreign Language Education at Community Colleges

THERE IS A RESURGENCE OF INTEREST IN FOREIGN LANGUAGE EDUCATION on the campuses of the nation's community colleges. Student registration in foreign language courses has increased, and new energies have focused on the development of foreign language programs and the role of foreign languages in the two-year college curriculum. Foreign language courses have traditionally been included as a component of the general education, transfer curriculum at two-year colleges. New efforts are connecting foreign language courses more closely to other humanities areas and to other parts of the curriculum. Renewed interest in international education, global studies, and the requirements of language acquisition for a combination of programmatic and occupational purposes has led to a significant expansion in the number of languages taught, especially the less commonly taught languages. Concurrently, advanced courses in languages are being added to existing offerings. Finally, a wide array of study abroad programs are conducted by community colleges in connection with foreign language programs. This paper will review these developments and identify problems that affect the purposes and quality of foreign language education.

The number of student registrations in foreign language courses has increased dramatically in the past five years.[1] A recent survey of 2,797 two-year and four year colleges and universities conducted by the Modern Language Association shows an 18 percent increase in enrollment in language courses from 1986 to 1991. The bulk of this increase reflects increased enrollments in the nation's two-year

David A. Berry is Executive Director of the Community College Humanities Association (CCHA) and Professor of History at Essex County College, NJ. He gratefully acknowledges the helpful assistance of Gina Baldo, U.S. Surgical Corporation, International Sales; Anne Levig, Cambridge Community College, MN; Nanette Pascal, Richland College, TX; Robert Vitale, Miami-Dade Community College, FL; Hannie Voyles, Butte College, CA; and Laura Walker, Tulsa Junior College, OK.

colleges. Fall, 1990 enrollments surpassed the previous peak year of 1968, and continued the trend of the rising number of enrollments that had followed the decline of the 1970s. Over 870 two-year colleges reported foreign language enrollments in the 1990 survey accounting for 19.3% of all foreign language registrations in the nation in 1990. In two-year colleges, foreign language enrollments increased by 65,539 or over 40% in the period from 1986 to 1991![2]

Most of the foreign language enrollment in two-year colleges is in Spanish (133,823 or 59%), French (44,366 or 19%), and German (19,082 or 8%). Japanese (10,308 or 5%) is the next most commonly taught language, followed by Italian (8,325 or 3.6%), Chinese (3,506 or 1.5%), and Russian (3,475 or 1.5%). In descending order, American Sign Language (1,140), Latin (909), Hebrew (786), Portuguese (365), Arabic (423), Hawaiian (299), ancient Greek (283), Filipino (178), Vietnamese (169), and Korean (141) are also taught at two-year colleges, but to very small numbers of students. Other languages reported being taught include: Apache, Aramaic, Arapaho, Armenian, Blackfoot, Choctaw, Crow, Dakota-Lakota, Dutch, Modern Greek, Hungarian, Inupiaq, Kutenai, Navajo, Norwegian, Ojibwa, Polish, Salish, Samoan, Swedish, Tagalog, Urdu, Yiddish, and Yupik.

These data reflect both renewed attention focused on foreign language instruction by college faculty and administrators and increased student interest in areas that require mastery of languages other than English. A recent survey conducted by the Community College Humanities Association (CCHA) of 161 two-year colleges shows that there is a variety of responses to the problem of the design of foreign language education that can be conveniently grouped into three models.[3] These models are not mutually exclusive, and some colleges

[1]The report of the Modern Language Association's 1990 survey of enrollments in foreign languages appeared in the Spring 1992 issue of the *ADFL Bulletin*. The data cited here is used by permission.

[2]It must be noted, however, that part of this dramatic increase needs to be attributed to demographic changes.

[3]Technical colleges do not offer foreign languages, except in rare cases, such as Nashville State Technical Institute which offers one section of Spanish I. The course can satisfy a humanities or general elective requirement. Foreign language courses are commonly defined by technical college administrators as courses to be offered only in transfer degree programs. There does not seem to be a clear rationale for this since the utility of foreign language study can be made for a number of occupational and/or technical programs. At the same time, many community colleges offer noncredit versions of foreign language courses.

actively pursue several programs simultaneously. Each institution does tend to emphasize one model in its foreign language education component, although ideally, the best features of each approach could be joined in an integrative program.

The first model might be termed the "language acquisition" or "traditional" model of foreign language education. Most respondents to the CCHA survey fit this model. In this case the college offers between one to four foreign languages, usually Spanish, French, and German, and, perhaps, one language that serves a particular, local need, such as Navajo (offered at Northland Pioneer College, AZ), or Japanese (offered at Everett Community College, WA, which houses a Nippon Business Institute). Ojibwe, for example, is not only emphasized at Arrowhead Community College, MN, but an Ojibwe Specialist Program resulting in an Associate in Arts degree is offered to train Native American students to teach Ojibwe language and culture. In the typical case the languages are offered primarily for students in the Associate in Arts degree transfer program. Generally six credits (two semesters) of foreign language course work is required, but occasionally up to twelve credits is required (e.g. Union County College, NJ). Foreign language acquisition is considered valuable in its own right,[4] and as an important first step in the careers of students who intend to pursue advanced degree in fields requiring foreign language competence. For these reasons the foreign language requirement is included in the Associate in Arts degree for transfer programs.

Two semesters of study at the beginning levels is sufficient to accomplish only the lowest levels of language competence. There is a precipitous drop in enrollments after the first year of language study. Few students get to the third year, or advanced level, of foreign language study. At some institutions only a few students pursue the Associate in Arts degree. Many more students take courses of study in the Associate in Science and Associate in Applied Science degrees and still

---

[4]Ernest Boyer argued in *Common Learning: A Carnegie Colloquium on General Education* that "The study of a *second* language is particularly important, not just because of its direct utility but also because such a study helps students view language freshly and see how language reflects cultural values and traditions." (p. 124); and Lynne V. Cheney notes in *American Memory*, "Studying a second language gives us greater mastery over our own speech, helps us shape our thoughts with greater precision and our expressions with greater eloquence. Studying a foreign language also provides insight into the nature of language itself, into its power to shape ideas and experience." (p. 13)

transfer to four-year institutions. Some thought needs to be given to the question of requiring foreign language courses in these degree programs. Students in technical and occupational fields, are generally not required to take foreign language courses, yet arguments for foreign language requirements apply to these students as well.

The second model, termed the "humanities program model," seeks to design a humanities program in which courses in a foreign language and the study of culture are joined in a common purpose. There are varying ways in which this is accomplished. The most common method is for instructors to stress the teaching of culture along with the language. The study of cultures and societies other than one's own has long been recognized by educators as a fundamental component of a liberal education. In the Renaissance, Montaigne warned of the dangers of provincialism when he wrote, "We all call barbarism that which does not fit in with our usages. And indeed, we seem to have no other standard of truth and reason but the example and model of the opinions and usages of the country we live in. There we always see the perfect religion, the perfect government, the perfect and accomplished manner of doing things." (Rice, p. 75)

Like the Renaissance humanists who learned Greek or Hebrew, advocates of this model stress the importance of the ability to read the written culture of peoples distant in time or place. Lynne V. Cheney, Chairman of the National Endowment for the Humanities (NEH), stressed the importance of a two-year foreign language requirement (12 semester hours) that builds on prior high school study so that "Students can begin to experience in the original, rather than through translation, profound and beautiful works that show how other people live and what they value." (Cheney, p. 29) One NEH-funded project, Academic Alliances in Languages and Literature, aims to increase the number of courses at the high school and college levels that teach foreign languages through the study of literary texts. Other colleges, such as Butte College, CA and Richland College, TX have designed special "classics cluster" programs that integrate foreign language courses with courses in history and literature. At Butte College, for example, a Certificate in Classical Studies is offered to students who complete two courses in Latin, one course in ancient Greek, and one course in Greco-Roman culture. The historical and literary content of all three courses is carefully coordinated by the instructor, and, if the student is enrolled in the college honors program, which is often the case, a philosophy course is also taken.

This model slights the importance of communicative skills in foreign language acquisition. Moreover, it is not always the case that students can master, let alone enjoy, even "simple" texts after only one or two semesters of study of a foreign language. Several colleges, however, offer upper level literature courses taught in one of the "traditional" languages. Frederick Community College, MD offers "Special Topics in French Literature" which is taught exclusively in French. Finally, at least one college, Oakton Community College, IL places an emphasis on foreign language education that extends to faculty development. A number of opportunities are provided for faculty, full and part-time, staff, and administrators to meet regularly to learn to speak another language and the "culture that is embedded in language."[5]

A third model is dominated by a new emphasis on the international education curriculum and on increasing numbers of students entering career or occupational programs that strongly recommend or require foreign language skills (e.g. Spanish for medical secretaries, or Japanese for business majors). The key term here is *skills*, i.e. the ability of a student to *use* a foreign language in a variety of practical applications. Colleges adopting this model often offer a wide array of foreign languages in both credit and non-credit formats. The primary emphasis is on language acquisition for conversational application; the skills of listening, speaking and reading are stressed. While at first glance this model seems to share a great deal with the humanities program model, this approach is driven by the demands of international business, international affairs, and the globalization of the world economy. Jerry Gaff, in his treatment of global studies perspectives in the curriculum, has noted that students need foreign language capability because "Americans need to speak foreign languages in order to serve the nation's interests, including peace, diplomacy, trade, environmental quality, and others. And larger numbers of foreign travelers and foreign products provide reminders of our linguistic limitations." (pp. 94–95) The International Language Center at Tulsa Junior College, OK and the International Language Institute at Richland College, TX are extremely successful examples of this model. The Richland College Institute aims to enable learners "to use the language in functional contexts and authentic cultural settings. Hence, for a language pro-

[5]From a report to CCHA by Margaret and Linda Korbel, Oakton Community College, IL, December 13, 1991.

gram to be effective, it must respond to the expectations for communicative competence. Language proficiency implies going beyond grammatical and lexical study at the sentence level to reach a general discourse competence in real-life situations."[6] Tulsa Junior College offers 14 languages to over 3,500 students each year, and the International Language Center has served over 10,000 students since its founding in 1987. The languages taught include ESL,[7] French, German, Spanish, Italian, American Sign Language, Arabic, Chinese, Greek, Hebrew, Japanese, Latin, Portuguese (Brazilian), and Russian. Both colleges rely on faculty training by the American Council on the Teaching of Foreign Languages (ACTFL) in proficiency-based teaching techniques. Faculty spend long hours interviewing students according to ACTFL proficiency guidelines, and in the case of Richland College, faculty helped to train French and Spanish teachers from Dallas area schools. French and Spanish courses at Richland College have been adapted to proficiency standards and to assessment and evaluation procedures; also, the use of new sophisticated laboratory equipment to test oral proficiency and to teach culture has been implemented. Each of the Tulsa Junior College's international language laboratories is equipped with a computerized electronic system in order to handle simultaneous instruction in 24 languages. Other colleges have invested in the state-of-the-art laboratory, including Florida Community College at Jacksonville and Central Piedmont Community College, NC. The certification program at Tulsa Junior College has encouraged students from area high schools to build on previous language study and to continue their training at appropriate levels, rather than to begin anew at Tulsa Junior College. In this way, language proficiency certification helps to increase student enrollment in advanced courses and, possibly, to seek degrees and/or certificates. The irony, of course, is that foreign language training ought not be postponed until college. Fred Hechinger, in his essay "The High School-College Connection," observed that "missing the opportunity of teaching a foreign language to children at age seven or eight or

[6]From a description of the "Program Philosophy" of the International Language Institute, Richland College, provided by Nanette Pascal.

[7]English as a Second Language (ESL) is not a foreign language per se, although it is often classified with foreign languages (e.g. the Center for the Study of Community Colleges at UCLA). ESL departments or instructors may or may not be administratively grouped with foreign language departments or instructors.

even younger places an unnecessary and unproductive mental burden on the teenagers or undergraduates or graduate students who, for the first time, try to cope with what would have been hardly any effort at all if it had been begun at the proper level of education. Equally wasteful is the teaching of foreign languages in elementary school, dropping it from the curriculum in junior or high school, and then, five or six years later, at the time of the graduate dissertation, suddenly requiring and expecting that a student pick up the language that he or she dropped so long ago." (p. 124)

The majority of instructors at Tulsa Junior College are part-time. Only six are full-time. These instructors meet weekly with the director of the International Language Center to develop instructional strategies which they, in turn, present to the adjunct faculty through an instructional development series. They also develop proficiency examinations and are responsible for syllabus and textbook adoptions.

In recognition of its relation to the Tulsa business community, the Tulsa World Trade Association named Tulsa Junior College the 1991 "International Achiever" for its commitment to educating Tulsans for the international economy. In this model of foreign language education, "culture" is likely to mean "business etiquette" and "dining difference," not historical tradition and major literary texts. The *French In Action* and *Destinos: An Introduction to Spanish* programs, produced by the Annenberg/CPB Project, are materials that seem to work well with this approach, for they are designed "to make language and culture come alive," and "to help students develop communicative proficiency—listening, speaking, reading and writing."[8] The emphasis is on listening and speaking. In a similar fashion, the editor of the fourth edition of a standard French text, *Parole et Pensee*, announced, "This book is intended as an aid in teaching beginning students to understand, speak, read, and write French. Listening, understanding, and speaking are of primary importance, and writing should not be allowed to come first, or to take the place of the audiolingual aspects of language." (Lenard, p. xvii)

Community college language administrators are proud of their "hands on," utilitarian approach to language instruction. One administrator, responding to the CCHA survey, pointedly compared his department with area four-year departments, noting that community

---

[8]Taken from the 1990 sheet announcing the *Destinos* television course, videocassettes, and print materials.

colleges had the ability to dedicate themselves totally to foreign language teaching without the "inconvenience" of teaching, say, literature. He said his faculty did teach the culture, they did teach literature, but the emphasis was on learning a language. The central question for prospective foreign language instructors, he said, was "How will you excite students to learn the language?"

Many community colleges offer study abroad programs. A great number, such as Miami-Dade Community College, FL which has both short, five- to six-week programs in Italy and France and semester-long programs in Spain, France, and Mexico, use existing consortia, in this case the 180 member College Consortium for International Studies (CCIS).[9] Additional community college sponsors for CCIS study abroad programs include Brookdale Community College, NJ, Erie Community College, NY, Rockland Community College, NY, Ocean County College, NJ, Mohegan Community College, CT, Broward Community College, FL, Westchester Community College, NY, Broome Community College, MA, Cape Cod Community College, MA, Mattatuck Community College, CT, and Jamestown Community College, NY. Other colleges have developed their own study abroad programs. Tulsa Junior College, under the auspices of the International Campus Program, will have three groups studying abroad in 1992: a business group and a humanities group in London and Germany, and English language groups in Austria and Germany. Emphasis is placed on the development of international awareness skills. Rockland Community College hosts a Center for International Studies and sponsors foreign study in London and in Israel. In addition, independent study and enrollment in courses at overseas universities are available. Study abroad programs provide experiences that will change students' affective attitudes. When this is the primary purpose of study abroad programs, the connections to foreign language acquisition and to the study of another culture are seriously weakened. There are cases where study abroad programs are not much more than travel tours.

Unfortunately, most community college study abroad programs are of a particularly short duration, rarely longer than three weeks. While these programs are certainly valuable, some effort ought to be made to increase the length of study abroad to at least one semester, or

---

[9]The host institution for the CCIS program is the Institute for American Universities, chartered by the Board of Regents of the State University of New York.

ideally, for even a longer period, although cost is certainly one of the major limiting factors. Casper College, WY boasts a modest scholarship for foreign travel, and other colleges might follow suit by attempting to secure funds dedicated to study abroad programs. In addition, the range of countries targeted for study abroad programs ought to be expanded to include more areas outside the well-traveled paths to England, France, and Mexico. Finally, efforts need to be made to ensure that study abroad courses and programs of study are integrated into a student's course of study at his home college.

In addition to study abroad programs, some community colleges have forged sister college partnerships. Tulsa Junior College, for example, is negotiating an agreement with a college in Utsunomiya, Japan. Special language classes are being organized for community residents who will be hosting Japanese visitors and/or visiting Utsunomiya.

All areas of the two-year college curriculum are affected by issues of foreign language education. Academic policies and the design of new programs need to be carried out in coherent and carefully designed ways in order to ensure the long-term success of existing and new programs.

BIBLIOGRAPHY

Boyer, Ernest. *Common Learning: A Carnegie Colloquium on General Education*. Washington, D.C.: The Carnegie Foundation for the Advancement of Teaching, 1981.

Brod, Richard I. "Foreign Language Enrollments in U.S. Institutions of Higher Education–Fall 1986" *ADFL Bulletin*, 1988, Vol. 19, No. 2.

Brod, Richard I. "Foreign Language Enrollments in U.S. Institutions of Higher Education–Fall 1990" *ADFL Bulletin*—forthcoming.

Cheney, Lynne V. *American Memory*. Washington, D.C.: National Endowment for the Humanities, 1987.

Cheney, Lynne V. *50 Hours: A Core Curriculum for College Students*. Washington, D.C.: National Endowment for the Humanities, 1989.

Gaff, Jerry G. *General Education Today*. San Francisco: Jossey-Bass Inc., 1983.

Hechinger, Fred. "The High School-College Connection" *Common Learning*, 1981. Washington, D.C.: The Carnegie Foundation for the Advancement of Teaching, p. 124.

Lambert, Richard D. *International Studies and the Undergraduate.* Washington, D.C.: American Council on Education, 1989.

Lenard, Yvone, ed. *Parole et Pensee.* New York: Harper and Row, Publishers, 1982.

Rice, E. *The Foundations of Early Modern Europe.* New York: Norton, 1970.

Anne Levig, Professor of Foreign Languages, Cambridge Community College, MN, discusses the Foreign Language Education Policy Statement at the 1992 AACC convention.

Laura Walker, Director, International Language Center, Tulsa Junior College, OK, comments on the Foreign Language Education Policy Statement at the 1992 AACC convention.

Fe Pittman Brittain

Making the Most of the Articulation Process

Introduction

Cross-cultural understanding and foreign language skills are not only the mark of an educated person today, but it is probable that they will be requisites for economic survival tomorrow. At a time when the nation's youth need learning opportunities that will qualify them for work in a global economy, we must find the will and the means whereby foreign language programs throughout the nation respond to the call for effective improvement.

Educators, scholars, government officials and members of the business community agree that foreign language skills are not adequate for promoting the nation's political and business objectives around the world. Global interdependency compels us to confront the reality of our need to study and understand the cultures, economies and politics of other countries and how these impact the United States.

The gravity of the situation is such that the American Council on Education recently issued a statement supporting foreign language education as a priority educational objective for the nation. The report, entitled *What We Can't Say Can Hurt Us: A Call for Foreign Language Competence by the Year 2000*, prescribed these recommendations:

1. Continuity in language learning should take place throughout the educational process.
2. Language competence should be an educational outcome.
3. Institutional initiatives are needed that will facilitate the process of language learning for students and faculty.

Fe Pittman Brittain, Ph.D., is Chair of the Foreign Language Department at Pima Community College, East Campus, AZ.

To attain these objectives, a commitment to the review, revision, and implementation of an articulation process among high schools, community colleges, and universities is essential. This commitment should be extended to a recommendation of a similar process between primary and secondary schools if the system is to provide a smooth transition in language study for all students. Indeed, the very meaning of articulation is "joining", and here it is extended to all levels of instruction and to the common continuing goals and objectives in which all levels participate.

This paper addresses the current problems impeding articulation in foreign language education, and it proposes several strategies for making articulation workable and successful. We must find ways to connect the various levels of language learning so that our teaching, and consequently our learning, is effective, efficient, and geared to meet the changing needs of our nation and our world.

CURRENT PROBLEMS OF ARTICULATION

Performance Standards

There is an absence of performance standards with clear-cut goals and objectives adaptable to all learning environments. These stan-

Fe Pittman Brittain at the AACC Foreign Language Education Roundtable, Washington, D.C.

dards are necessary for creating the means to assess foreign language proficiency. Language teachers and professors must be told, "Here is the performance standard. It is your responsibility to implement this in your environment with your students." Such a performance standard provides the people who operate the system with the opportunity to build it creatively. It will yield not only quality language-learning experiences, but also the incentive to achieve even higher performance standards.

Assessment Instruments

The lack of agreement about state and national language proficiency tests inhibits the development of accurate assessment instruments. The current lack of adequate and effective evaluation affects other areas as well: student selection and placement, teaching methods, and the relationship between languages learned in the classroom and those learned in "non-academic" environments. As well, efficient assessment is necessary not only for effective education in schools, but for the schools' rapport with employers and their commercial expectations of language proficiency in their employees.

University Language Requirements for Admission

The recent surge of interest in foreign language has resulted in the reinstatement of foreign language requirements at many institutions of higher learning. (Klee and Rogers, 1989; Schulz, 1991) This higher entry-level foreign language requirement excludes certain students from enrolling in or transferring into foreign language programs because no effort has been made to coordinate/articulate the high school programs with these changes in foreign language requirements at the college level. These more stringent requirements, understandable and deemed necessary by post-secondary institutions, impact widely upon the community colleges which must provide language courses for students caught in the proverbial "middle" and, at the same time, be certain that their programs are providing the background to insure student success at the more advanced levels of language study. All this is required of the two-year college curriculum in a period of no-growth and fiscal restraint.

SOME STEPS TOWARD SOLUTIONS

Performance Standards

The foreign language teaching profession should establish a set of performance standards adaptable to *all* learning environments. This requires research involving the classroom teacher and collaborative efforts between high schools, two-year colleges and universities. Input from language instructors at all levels is needed to create a realistic appraisal of what is being taught and how it is being learned in foreign language classes. Through careful collaborative research we can determine what are the best ways to organize the curriculum, how language acquisition occurs in various classroom settings, and what methodologies are most successful at which levels of language development. It is essential that researchers and practitioners have opportunities to communicate with one another if meaningful theory-building in language learning is to take place. (Bailey et al, 1991)

Assessment, Evaluation, and Performance Standards

The need to develop acceptable, valid, and reliable tests and data collection instruments is also crucial to the theory-building process in research. (Bailey et al, 1991) In other words, these two critical areas, evaluation and performance standards, are closely tied to one another. Useful theories pertaining to language learning and acquisition cannot be reliably investigated without these proper tools. As Renate Schulz points out, none of the present second language acquisition theories offers a complete and coherent explanation of this extremely complex process. However, as a practitioner, Schulz "sees the prime value of theory and research in their potential for leading us to possible practical implications and applications to improve teaching and learning." (Schulz, 1991) This is precisely why we need participation from the classroom teacher, the person involved in the day-to-day process of language education. It is vital that the foreign language articulation process become a reality. Only then can we accomplish meaningful research in second language acquisition theories—research that can result in clearer understanding of the learning process and ultimately, better products.

University and College Language Requirements

If the foreign language teaching profession, through collaboration on all levels, achieves accepted means of testing and agreed-upon performance standards, a major problem for students and faculty at the college level will be greatly alleviated. Students will not arrive at the college or university with little or no foreign language preparation and yet be expected to demonstrate effective communicative skills plus cultural awareness in as little as two years. As Pankenier pointed out, "We delude ourselves [and our students] if we think that merely requiring a year or two of language instruction in college is going to produce significant improvement in the cultural or linguistic sophistication of our graduates or enhance our ability to compete internationally. If we are as serious about the importance of linguistic sophistication as we profess to be, then language study ought to be required from elementary school onward, just as the study of mathematics and writing is." (1990, p. B3)

Swaffar posits, ". . . regardless of method, the average performance at the end of two years of high school or college was not high enough to encourage expectations that students would be able to use that second language in some practical way." (1989, p. 55) Swaffar also refers to John Carroll's well-known study done in 1967 which revealed the fallacy of unreasonable expectations: mastery of surface second language was *not* feasible even in four years.

There are indications that many universities are, indeed, taking the steps necessary to enforce language study in the high schools by establishing higher entrance requirements. The process would benefit students more, however, if through collaborative efforts the course of study were defined and agreed upon, developing language competency to a level that would assure student success at the university and college levels.

FACTORS FAVORING AN EFFECTIVE ARTICULATION PROCESS

The landscape of education, unfortunately, is littered with the bones of unsuccessful attempts to articulate courses and programs between the community college and the university. A significant factor in these disappointments is the lack of understanding as to what the articulation problems are, as well as the absence of agreement about performance standards. The workability and the success of an effective articulation effort can be directly influenced if the following steps are undertaken:

1. Review of the articulation history between institutions, both within the state and within the academic community;
2. Adoption of a prescribed performance standard in which levels of language proficiency are determined;
3. Development of accepted instruments of evaluation which can be easily and economically administered at different levels of language study;
4. Establishment of a mechanism whereby counterparts from each of the institutions are directly in touch with each other;
5. Reaching an agreement between institutions that, while preserving institutional autonomy, language courses and programs, will adhere to prescribed performance standards; and
6. Reinforcement of an unwritten, but clearly and mutually held, belief in the importance of communication and mutual respect.

ARTICULATION AND CONTEMPORARY NEEDS

The first steps in this endeavor to respond to the national need for effective improvement in foreign language education are to adopt performance standards for language proficiency and to articulate language courses and programs throughout the system.

Harold Hodgkinson, in his reports on demographic changes in the United States, points out the sweeping changes that we need to prepare for in the near future. More of our clients in education will be minorities and women. The major responsibility for preparing these students for successful completion of advanced degrees is falling to the community colleges. By far, the majority of first-time minority, women and non-traditional freshmen select two-year institutions at which to begin their college education. Thus, articulation between community colleges and universities will greatly increase the probability of student success. Hodgkinson also maintains that now is the wrong time to orient schools toward serving as screening mechanisms, and that since 82% of the workforce between now and the year 2000 will be a combination of females, minorities and immigrants, our goals should be to educate everyone to their highest potential, not "weed" them out of higher education. Everyone will need a sophisticated education to successfully operate in the high-tech global village of the future.

It may appear that this paper, with its emphasis on establishing foreign language performance standards and assessment instruments, is in direct contrast with Hodgkinson's protest against screening mechanisms. This is certainly not the case, as this paper recommends that we develop common levels of expected proficiency or language competency, and the means to evaluate such, is not to "weed out" the losers or to create an elite group of winners, but rather, it is to provide a learning situation in which every student can succeed. Heidi Byrnes, in her presentation to the Georgetown University Round Table on Language and Linguistics entitled "The Learner-Curriculum-Testing Connection: Who is in Charge?," stressed the importance of interpreting testing data so that it can be used to enhance and improve the process of instruction and the foreign language curriculum, finding in the *product* of instruction, as ascertained through testing, means of improving the *process* of instruction. She posited that if we do not enhance future learning through the enterprise of testing, we are engaged in a fatalistic venture.

If language study is encouraged and accepted as an integral part of the curriculum from grade school through the university level, much of the current frustration and failure we see in students who encounter second language study for the first time at the college level will disappear. It is not in the best interest of students for us to separate "our" college level language program from "their" high school and elementary level language programs. In 1991, Senator Paul Simon repeated his strong belief that, "more than ever, Americans need foreign language fluency [and an appreciation of other cultures]." This cannot be accomplished in two years of college study. When Senator Simon visited Botswana, he was struck by the realization that their average fourth grader has four more years of foreign language study than the average college graduate in the United States.

The reality is that articulation through all levels of language learning is essential, not only to insure that all students have an opportunity to study language and culture over a period of several years, but also to prevent students from needlessly repeating the same materials and levels of language study throughout their educational careers.

The major mechanism for bringing together counterparts from many institutions is research. Research is also the major factor in developing sound theories regarding this complex phenomenon of language acquisition. Classroom-based second-language-acquisition research on testing, curriculum development, and expected competency levels can help us build good, solid articulation. Universities would greatly benefit the profession of language teaching if they encouraged cooperative research between institutions. There is much to share and investigate: recent second language acquisition theories, different methodologies, new materials, information on individual learning styles, to name a few. Graduate students, actively involved in these areas through their investigatory studies, should be given the opportunity to work with high school and elementary school language teachers, actively involved in the *process*. And who is in a better position to try these new ideas and processes than the classroom teacher, who very likely does not have the time to organize the statistics, background research, and the report itself? University and college professors, graduate and undergraduate students, high school and elementary teachers and their students, researchers, and administrators—What a synergetic combination this could be!

Conclusion

Effective articulation is, in one sense, the only path to cross-level improvement in language instruction. Each level depends on the other. Overall improvement in the effectiveness of language instruction which *will* produce, through progressive levels, language "graduates" who are capable of understanding, speaking, reading and writing a second language can only come through articulation from elementary school through college. A regional "pilot" program involving a public school district, a community college, and a university would provide a model for those who are looking to implement articulation activities in their environment.

Communication, collaborative efforts among professionals of all learning environments, as well as administrative commitment, are essential elements to ensure the success of any educational activity, program or project. Many among the "best and brightest" have contemplated what needs to be done to promote articulation in language studies. What we must do now is muster the will and determination to put these ideas into practice.

We live in a world of wide diversity, of extremely rapid change, and even more rapid communication. This communication must be clear; the communicators must be informed and responsible. Let us learn to talk to each other and to listen. Let us change the dictum so that it reads, "What we can say won't hurt us," and then let's *say* it.

BIBLIOGRAPHY

Bailey, Kathleen, Alice Omaggio Hadly, Sally Sieloff Magnan, and Janet Swaffar. "Priority: Research in the 1990s: Focus on Theory building, Instructional Innovation, and Collaboration." *Foreign Language Annals*, 1991, Vol. 24, No. 2, pp. 89–100.

Barnes, Betsy, Carol Klee, and Ray Wakefield. "A Funny Thing Happened on the Way to the Language Requirement." *ADFL Bulletin*, 1990, Vol. 22, No. 1, pp. 35–39.

Brod, Richard. "Reaction: Priorities for the Language Field in the United States." *Foreign Language Annals*, 1991, Vol. 24, No. 1, pp. 19–20.

Byrnes, Heidi. "Who is in Charge in the Learner-Curriculum-Testing Connection?" *Georgetown University Round Table on Languages and Linguistics 1989*. Georgetown University, 1989.

Byrnes, Heidi. "Addressing Curriculum Articulation in the Nineties: A Proposal." *Foreign Language Annals*, Sept. 1990, pp. 281–290.

Calderback, Mark and Muhammad Awwad. "Testing Oral Communication: Why and How?" *System: An International Journal of Educational Technology and Applied Linguistics*, 1988, Vol. 16, No. 1, pp. 49–59.

Chastain, Kenneth. *Toward a Philosophy of Second Language Learning and Teaching*. Boston: Heinle and Heinle, 1980.

Cummins, Patricia W. "School-College Articulation and Proficiency Standards: A Status Report." *ADFL Bulletin*, 1987, Vol. 19, No. 1, pp. 8–15.

Gandara, Patricia. "School and College Collaboration: An Introduction." *Thought and Action, The NEA Higher Education Journal*, 1991, Vol. VII, No. 1, pp. 91–92.

Hammerly, Hector. *An Integrated Theory of Language Teaching and Its Practical Consequences*, Volume 2. Blaine, WA: Second Language Publications, 1985.

Hodgkinson, Harold L. "The Context of the 21st Century: Civics and Citizenship." Center for Demographic Policy, Washington, D.C.: 1988.

Jeffries, Sophie and Irmgard C. Taylor. "Articulation in New York State: Toward a Model for a National Foreign Language Curriculum." *ADFL Bulletin*, 1991, Vol. 23, No. 1, pp. 22–27.

Klee, Carol A. and Elizabeth S. Rogers. "Status of Articulation: Placement, Advanced Placement Credit, and Course Options." *Hispania*, 1989, Vol. 72, Sept., pp. 763–771.

Pankenier, David W. "Foreign Language Requirements at the College Level Do Not Work." *The Chronicle of Higher Education*, 1990, Vol. 5, Dec., pp. B2–3.

Schulz, Renate A. "Second Language Acquisition Theories and Teaching Practice: How Do They Fit?" *The Modern Language Journal*, 1991, Vol. 75, No. 1, pp. 17–26.

Simon, Paul. "Priority: Public Relations. A Decade of Change to a Decade of Challenge." *Foreign Language Annals*, 1991, Vol. 24, No. 1, pp. 13–18.

Swaffar, Janet K. "Curricular Issues and Language Research: The Shifting Interaction." *ADFL Bulletin*, 1989, Vol. 20, No. 3, pp. 54–60.

JOHN UNDERWOOD

Uses of Technology to Teach Foreign Languages at Community Colleges

I WAS INVITED TWO YEARS AGO TO MAKE A CONSULTING VISIT TO THE foreign language department of a community college in eastern Washington state. Their situation was typical: the Dean had offered funds to set up a lab if they could come up with an innovative proposal. A faculty committee had visited other schools, examined existing facilities on campus, and had written a proposal. When it was approved, however, the department realized there was another, more serious, problem facing them: despite the claims of their own proposal, there was no real agreement as to what they wanted to do. By the time I went to speak to them they were filled with ideas but lacked a clear or convincing reason for pursuing any of them. They said, "If we just bought some videotapes, everyone would be happy. But the reason for a full-blown lab is not so clear."

The technology quandary is a familiar phenomenon in language departments at all levels. There are actually three parts to the puzzle. One is cost: creating or updating a traditional language lab can be a major investment in both hardware and software at a time when budgets are tight. The issue of funding is closely tied to the question of purpose. If a department is to spend that much money and time designing and setting up a new system, they need to be sure they are going in the right direction. And tied to this issue is the sensitive matter of differences in faculty interest and motivation. It is human nature to be curious about new ways of doing things, but it is equally human to feel "it's all very nice, but somehow it's not me," or "I'll never find time to do *that*." Clearly, the most useful approach to all three parts of the puzzle is a convincing demonstration that technol-

John Underwood is Associate Professor of Spanish/Linguistics at Western Washington University.

ogy can have a very real, useful and pedagogically defensible place in language teaching. This paper will primarily address this last issue and make recommendations to two-year colleges for proceeding—gingerly, if need be—through this technological wonderland.

LANGUAGE TEACHING TODAY

The language teacher is no longer seen as a dispenser of knowledge, an expert holding forth at the front of the room, but rather as a facilitator or catalyst in a world of exploratory and cooperative learning. The teacher creates an environment in which learning can take place, an atmosphere that is comfortable rather than anxiety-producing, where students are "safe" to experiment and make mistakes, and where activities encourage them to use the language to communicate personal messages with their peers, to solve mutual problems (such as "A + B" pictures with missing information), and ultimately to see the language as a tool rather than as an object to be committed to memory a piece at a time.

The role of technology in this picture has been the subject of some debate. There are those of us who have argued for some time that computer-assisted language learning (CALL) has tended to focus on the more mechanical and less global aspects of language and is therefore inconsistent with current methodological theory and classroom practice.[1] (Underwood, 1984; Higgins & Johns, 1984) Technology, it was argued, can be and should be used in more creative and communicative ways: task-based activities, simulated dialogues, and global activities centered on the overall meaning of the language. None of these exercises are beyond the scope of CALL programming, they are merely more difficult and more time-consuming to implement. Meanwhile, other observers argued that precisely since there was no longer as much emphasis in the classroom on the more formal aspects of language, the lab would, in fact, be a good place to have students focus on them, at their own level, and at their own speed. Today,

---

[1] For much of the following discussion I will assume a three-way distinction in types of language exercises, whether in the classroom or on the computer: (1) mechanical exercises are those in which the forms are manipulated without concern for the meaning of the sentences; (2) meaningful exercises require understanding the content of the material, but without any real exchange of information; (3) communicative exercises contain some sort of information gap and hence can only be completed through the sharing of real information.

both kinds of activities can be found in the lab, although the drill-and-practice program still dominates (and has become surprisingly popular with students). Although the controversy has not been resolved, with today's increasing emphasis on the importance of video images in the lab, with or without the aid of a computer, including interactive video, the question of whether the computer itself can teach language has lost some of its urgency.

TECHNOLOGY IN THE LAB

The traditional audio lab has tape decks in parallel booths and a monitoring station at the front where the instructor can choose the program for the students and overhear what is being said in individual booths. In the classic audio routine, students listen to the master track, record their own response, then replay both the master's and their own for comparison. As early as the 1960's this practice was criticized as being too mechanical and artificial, with too much emphasis on pronunciation, and not enough meaningful context or opportunity for thought. Studies only confirmed the obvious: that students seldom take the time to record, play back, and compare their responses, and are not particularly good at self-correction. (Higgins, 1975) By the 1970's many labs had fallen into disuse. One innovation saved it from complete mothballing: the discovery that it could be put to good use for a more meaningful type of practice, the listening comprehension exercise. Textbook publishers began offering tapes accompanied by student workbooks designed more to focus on listening tasks than to stimulate speaking. This type of audio lab activity continues to be common today, though in most cases it is no longer practiced in the lab itself but on the student's own portable cassette player at home or on the road; this dramatic shift of audio use from the lab to the student's own environment is known in the profession as the "walkman phenomenon."

ENTER THE COMPUTER

In the 1970's we begin to see another important shift in the lab. The introduction of the microcomputer (especially, at first, the Apple II and the IBM PC) made it possible to put a stand-alone computer in each student station. Early uses were necessarily homegrown and rather crude—no help, no feedback, three tries and you're out—and the computer was always right. In fact, CALL programs tended to suffer from the same drawbacks as the early audio lab: they were boring, not highly contextualized, not well integrated into the curriculum, and not designed to strengthen any communicative aspect of language. Experimentation led to a number of more workable models for lab practice. These will here be described in terms of a few standard generic categories. From these the reader will be able to judge how much—or how little—the computer may contribute to the student's learning.

Drill and Practice

"Classical" grammar drill-and-practice, the most common use of the computer for language learning, requires manipulation of words or sentences where the answer is controlled (such as in "dehydrated sentences," fill-ins, and so forth.). The pedagogical value of such programs will depend largely on the quality of the error analysis the program can provide, if any. (Early programs responded with little more than "Wrong, try again.") A somewhat more enlightened version of drill-and-practice will try to point the confused student in the direction of the right form by highlighting the wrong word and hinting at the problem. The hint may range from a purely grammatical statement ("Masculine or feminine?") to a reference to the context ("You mention her. Is Charles a girl?"). Note that the student's attention is necessarily focused on the form of the words rather than on their meaning, and that the feedback from the program is usually phrased in terms of form, such as parts of speech and tenses. Criticism of CALL has centered on this lack of context or semantic content; it is normally not necessary to understand what the sentences mean in order to respond correctly.

Text Reconstruction

In reconstruction programs, the basic idea is derived from the cloze exercise, passages in which a certain number of words have been deleted and must be replaced by the student. Reconstruction is an example of a more contextualized and global type of activity, since the meaning of the passage is an important clue to the identity of the missing words. The computer serves as facilitator and aide; when students are stumped, they can ask for a hint such as the first letter of the word, a translation, or some other clue. The extreme example of a cloze exercise is the Storyboard program, in which the student reads a passage, watches as the computer replaces each word with a blank, then reconstructs it word by word. A combination of context, structure, vocabulary and memory will aid the student in recovering the words. Hence, it is argued that though it is not a communicative activity, it is definitely a meaningful one.

Simulation and Games

Just as pilots learn to fly in computer-controlled flight simulators requiring them to use real piloting skills, language students can participate in a make-believe world in which they must use the target language to get by. At the simplest level, this microworld exists only in text on the screen, as in the classic adventure game ("You are in a forest, there is a house to the left. Which direction do you wish to move?"). More elaborate versions use graphics or videodisc images to simulate their microworld. One of the most promising simulation projects is *No recuerdo*, an interactive videodisc project for Spanish developed at MIT as part of the Athena Project. Immersed in the on-screen world of an amnesiac scientist, the student uses the computer to explore the environment, examine objects, and "talk" to the characters by typing in questions or answers in response to what takes place on the screen. Much of this practice is clearly communicative in nature, since information is being exchanged.

Tool Programs

Sometimes called "serendipity programs" because they were designed for purposes other than CALL (e.g., word processing, spelling checkers, databases), various types of tool software have proven useful to the language student. Word-processing programs, especially those which include a foreign-language dictionary and/or spelling checker, can do much to help students refine their writing skills, including punctuation, spelling, and awareness of morphological detail. Data-base programs have been used as reference tools, providing an on-line source of information about grammatical forms or lexical relationships. Several language departments have experimented with using either the local-area network (LAN) in their lab or their campus computer-mail system to have students practice writing and "mailing" messages or short compositions to each other and to their instructor. The medium of electronic mail seems to encourage students to write more freely and to use a wider range of language functions in their messages (requests, complaints, confirmation, etc.).

CALL: LOOKING AHEAD

The preceding view of what has been done in CALL is by no means the whole picture of what can be done with computers in language learning. Much of the potential of language learning technology can be surmised from work under way in other fields of computational research. One promising direction would entail borrowing from artificial intelligence strategies to make CALL programs "smarter" and more "human." "Intelligent tutoring systems" may not only know certain information about the activity (such as knowledge of the language and the context, or story line, in which the language is being practiced), they may also learn important details about the student during the session. Based on an analysis of errors and restarts, the system can determine what students know, what they do not know, and what they need to do next. (Underwood, 1989)

Central to the artificially intelligent system is the notion of parsing. Parsing programs have complicated algorithms for deciphering the user's sentence and determining its meaning or structure—or both. At the simplest level, parsers can correctly identify the parts of speech to which words belong, something akin to drawing a sentence diagram. At the other end, parsers can "understand" language well enough to read a story and summarize it. In an experimental language learning program developed as part of Athena, the student uses typed-in German commands to order a "poltergeist" to move objects around in the graphic mini-world on the screen. By parsing the student's commands, the program can determine the intended meaning behind each statement and act upon it by causing the appropriate change in the graphics. (Kramsch, 1985) As promising as such programs sound, as yet there are very few such systems which are available to the teachers who need them.

VIDEO

Perhaps due to a certain inevitable disenchantment with the limitations and frustrations of CALL (including the technical difficulty in achieving anything other than the most rudimentary program), in the late 1980's videotape recorders came to be seen as a more promising use of technology. The reasons were obvious—video offers an authentic language sample presented in a culturally-rich context in which students both see and hear the world of the second language speaker. What is more, video equipment and tapes were relatively inexpensive and simple to use, requiring no programming or troublesome software. With the growing popularity and standardization of the VHS videocassette recorder, each booth in the lab could have independently-controllable color video. For a relatively nominal expense, the department could acquire a library of foreign films for students to watch and study.

Thus, the language lab entered the age of video, in which the use of the computer was not replaced, but rather supplemented by the rich and colorful environment created by these visual images. New ways were found to present video material to the student, emphasizing careful preparation before viewing ("What do you think will happen next?"), comprehension checks, and using the material for language study. Teachers were encouraged to show and discuss manageable chunks of video rather than have the whole piece flash by without commentary. (Altman, 1990) Once the first glow of enthusiasm had waned, though, teachers realized that the real problem with video was not how to show it but what to show. There are hundreds of foreign films available on tape, yet few of them are accessible to first- or second-year students. Video packages from educational publishers usually consist of pedestrian travelogues or cultural samplers. Video clearinghouses such as the University of Iowa's Project for International Communication Studies (PICS) offer videotaped television programs in a variety of languages, programs which have been downloaded from international television satellites; the news stories and so forth are both authentic and recent, but they still suffer from the problem of accessibility, since neither the language nor the situation is familiar to the student.

SATELLITE TV/SATELLITE BROADCAST

The popularization of the satellite television dish has led to two very different applications in foreign language teaching. One is the use of a properly-aimed antenna dish to receive television signals from overseas (hence, foreign-language) transmitters. Language departments on the east coast can bring in live European broadcasts; with the difference in time, they can catch the nightly news from Paris or Madrid over breakfast in Baltimore. Departments using a satellite dish on the west coast cannot pick up Western Europe but receive constant programming from Mexico, French Canada, and the Soviet Union. No sooner had all this authentic foreign language material become available, however, when language departments realized they faced two thorny issues: what to do with all the hours of video coming in, and what legal rights—if any—they had to copy and use broadcast material.

The question of copyright is still very confused. Unless one negotiates with the overseas networks for more general rights,[2] off-air recordings may be used in the classroom for only ten days, and the tape may be kept for a maximum of 45 days. (Congressional Record, 1981) But even with permission to keep the material, there is still the enormous problem of monitoring what comes in from the satellite twenty-four hours a day, deciding what to down-load, copying it (on a multi-standard VCR, since most countries use a different television scanning system from ours), then determining how—or if—it can be presented to students. Because such material is only too authentic, some form of preview or comprehension materials will be needed to allow students more access to the video material. This considerable process of bringing the programming from airwaves to lab has proven to require more staffing than most departments can afford.

The second application of satellite dish technology is virtually the reverse process. To reach remote areas with little or no foreign language instruction, especially in the lesser-taught languages, university foreign language departments have begun transmitting instruction via satellite. The receiving institution needs only a satellite dish and sufficient television monitors in their classrooms. Because this use of technology centers on the transmission of instruction rather than on its enhancement—our underlying topic here—it will not be dealt with further.

Videodisc and Interactive Video

The search for good video material becomes acute when the medium is videodisc rather than videotape, for there are still only a

---

[2]It was in this manner that PICS obtained the license to copy and distribute European television programming to U.S. schools.

handful of useful foreign language discs available. Yet the interest in videodisc is strong, and it is growing. Its advantages are many, and they all have to do with control. With disc, each image in the moving picture is a single frame of video with a unique index number that enables it to be accessed quickly and precisely. The best tape players can only come close, within a few frames, and they may take ten times as long to get there. This gives the teacher a chance to use single frames of video as slides, to jump forward or back instantly to display or compare frames or moving sequences. And the picture quality of the single frame remains every bit as good as that of the moving sequence.

The videodisc player has one other advantage which accounts for its increasing popularity in education—it can be controlled by a computer. Assuming the player is equipped for external connections, and that the computer has a piece of software known as a "videodisc driver" which allows it to "talk" to the videodisc player, then the computer can be used as a "front end" to the video, much as the keyboard serves as the front end to the computer itself. This means that access to certain key frames, scenes, or lines of dialogue can be programmed into the computer in advance. The student then only has to click on a certain area or "button" on the computer screen to have it play or replay the scene or line of dialogue. The result is known as "interactive video" (IAV).

The potential of IAV is far-reaching. The problem of the accessibility of the language and context is virtually eliminated. Everything on the disc, everything that is seen and heard, can be viewed and reviewed by the student as often as is needed. In addition, the computer can ask a series of comprehension questions to aid in the student's understanding. Or it can provide an on-line glossary of key words, translations, an index of key characters in the story, grammar or culture notes, background readings, and so on. In its ability to freeze video on demand and expose its linguistic and cultural secrets, the computer has come into its own.

HYPERTEXT AND HYPERMEDIA

The concept of hypermedia is related to the earlier notion of "hypertext," a way of reading and interacting with text on the computer screen. A hypertext system allows users to select a segment of text on the screen (perhaps by pointing at it or clicking on it) and cause the text to open up to a footnote, a translation, bibliographical data, or some other related text or graphics. Nonsequential links between one document and another, or between one footnote and another, allow users to follow trails in any direction without losing their original context. Thus, each reader in effect creates a new document by chaining together fragments of text in a personal fashion. The result compels us to alter our notion of both the "text" and "reading." (Underwood, 1988)

For all its potential, hypertext is limited to words on the screen. However, if one links a hypertext system to other media (audio, video, graphics, animation), the result is a rich and powerful delivery system known as "hypermedia" or "multimedia." In the same way that hypertext can zoom open to reveal its inner secrets (by linking to other, related, text), hypermedia can open windows and take the "reader" out into the world. Hypermedia gives the student power over the environment: the power to explore a body of information without being constrained by the author's view of how it all fits together, the power to follow an idea as far as one's imagination, and the media, will allow. Picture a language activity based on a map of Spanish-speaking countries; clicking on any point on the map on the computer screen would invoke a full-color video image of that corner of the world. Or the user could "fly" over the map while the video monitor follows along with a continuous moving video sequence of what one would see below. Or the program could be used as a kind of data base, whereby the user types in the name of a country, city, river, or mountain, and it is then outlined on the map at the same time as a corresponding color photograph appears on the video screen, and a voice describes it in Spanish.

CD-ROM: Large-Scale Storage of Media

Adding to the hypermedia picture is the use of CD-ROM (compact disc-read only memory), a storage medium that closely resembles CD audio. The drawback of CD-ROM, as the name suggests, is that one cannot—at present—record on it. Its advantage is its nearly inconceivable storage capacity: one thin little disk can hold something in the neighborhood of 600 megabytes, enough to hold the complete works of Shakespeare and still have room for the Random House Encyclopedia. What CD-ROM offers the hypermedia system, then, is a place to store a nearly inexhaustible supply of foreign language material. Chunks of data, which can include text, audio, graphics and—in time—a limited amount of video, are up-loaded into the computer on demand. Here one meets the other disadvantage of CD-ROM—access is slow by the standards of today's computer. But the technology is changing quickly; a spinoff or hybrid version will soon offer greater video capacity, faster speed, and the crucial ability to record and erase material on the disk.

SOURCES OF SOFTWARE

In all this, we have been discussing various types of programs and materials as if they are all in place, ready for the using. The reality is considerably more complicated. Most software now in use in language labs was developed on the site to suit the needs of the local population. Apart from the obvious duplication of effort in proceeding in this manner, it stands to reason that no one department can come up with all of the techniques and strategies that would be possible if this were a more collective project. How did this happen? In moving toward computers, language departments eventually all made the same discovery—ready-made, off-the-shelf software would not suit their needs. Even if they purchased all the Word Attack, Hangman, and various other "drill-and-kill" programs available, instructors felt these would never justify their investment in the machines.

Since the first language software began appearing on the shelves, there has been a more or less continuous debate over the role of the teacher in the development of programs. While it is clear that any competent language teacher knows more about designing language materials than the computer specialists who have been writing the programs, it is also clear that few language teachers want to know much about programming. Writing code is an extremely labor-intensive business, best contracted out to computer professionals. In any case, there are now several alternatives to creating a program from the ground up. For example, rather than using a general-purpose programming language such as BASIC or Pascal, a teacher interested in developing CALL materials would be better off with one of the so-called "authoring systems" which have become available in the last few years. An authoring system is designed so that one does not need to handle the code at all. The teacher/author need only think about the content of the program—what it should say and where it should say it. The programming goes on behind the scenes, so to speak. Such systems are often referred to as "templates" since they contain all of the structure but none of the content.

THE LANGUAGE LAB OF THE FUTURE?

Where will the lab go from here? Attempting to predict future trends is risky at best. Early proponents of the language lab proclaimed noisily that these machines would prove to be the ultimate teacher's aide—a tireless drillmaster, a perfect pronunciation model, and a way to free the teacher for more intellectual pursuits in the classroom. The truth, of course, is that the lab very nearly did us in. Still, it is tempting to extrapolate from what we know to be possible to what could very soon be reality:

> Cris, a freshman student at a medium-sized urban junior college, is seated at a workstation in what used to be called the "language lab." Several things have changed, though. In front of her is a color screen on which appear computer graphics and text superimposed on video images, all of which Cris controls by the simple click of a mouse. Through her stereo earphones she hears the dialogue and music of the video program as well as the digitized voice of "Carlos," her computer and her personal tutor. In a natural voice and impeccable Castilian, Carlos questions her about the content of the opening scene in the current episode of the video story. Cris answers by speaking a few words into the miniature microphone in front of her. Carlos says he likes her answer, but suggests she listen again to what Pedro said at the beginning of the scene . . .

Cris is immersed in an authentic language experience. The Spanish she uses—and hears—is given life and meaning by the vivid context of the story taking place on the video before her, and by all the resources which she, and Carlos, have at their disposal: a pronouncing dictionary which can search through the dialogue and play back examples, a visual index of scenes to help her retrace her steps, "footnote" dialogue boxes on all important vocabulary, structure and culture items—as they occur. Carlos even knows how much Spanish Cris knows, how to speak to her and be understood, and how much she understands about the story. He carefully chooses his questions and his own vocabulary and structure so that at no point is Cris asked to participate in an activity for which she is not prepared, or which is too easy for her.

Although such a system is not yet presently in use in this form, most of the components are currently feasible. The fine-tuned recognition and understanding of Cris's speech is now possible on a small scale (hence the limitation to "a few words"). Carlos's understanding of her Spanish could be achieved by a high-speed parser, once the problem of speech recognition had been overcome. And his knowledge of Cris's level and needs merely imitates experimental intelligent tutoring systems now under development. The hardware in Cris's workstation is no longer a "tower" of separate components (computer, laserdisc player, CD-ROM, speakers, monitors, etc.). Because the computer contains a recordable/erasable optical storage drive, it can store audio, video, graphics, and text data indiscriminately and process it all at extremely high speed.

CONCLUSION

It is becoming increasingly apparent in the profession that the first two years of instruction can be crucial to students' ultimate success in the language—determining their attitude toward the language and toward language learning, their motivation to continue, and their linguistic foundation for later study. For this reason, the unique circumstances of community colleges make them in many ways an ideal environment for language instruction focusing on these crucial early years. And it is during this time that the use of technology can be vital.

Do we need technology? As is hopefully evident from the discussion above, there are any number of ways in which technological aids can help, even teach, the student. Even as we explore the appropriate uses for today's systems, the hardware gets faster, the software more sophisticated. But there are other reasons, having to do with the nature of our world, and the world which is coming. A generation is growing up which takes technology for granted. Some thirty million Nintendo games have been sold, and "as their players pass through the schools and their careers, they will demand no less technology in the world around them." (Apple Corporation's John Sculley in Borchardt, 1991) And we have moved beyond the question of whether computers will replace teachers: "Computers will not replace teachers, but teachers who use computers will replace teachers who don't." (DLI-Monterey's Ray Clifford in Borchardt, 1991) Hence, the real need in our colleges will not be for the machines, since these can only become easier to acquire, but for large-scale faculty training in both the use and development of technology-related materials. Departments will have to shift their faculty development energies from personal scholarship to the production of materials for the use of beginning and intermediate students.

As student demand for language instruction increases and staffing funds lag behind or even decrease, the need for well-conceived individualized instruction will become acute. Colleges are already using lab work to replace lost classroom contact hours. An otherwise staff-heavy intensive Spanish program, for example, can now dedicate fully fifty percent of student credit hours to video and software programs. With integrated self-study materials, the department can design a wide-ranging and flexible program for a fraction of the usual cost. The motivated learner will be able to achieve a basic communicative competence through an individualized program supported by a textbook, audio and video tapes, and the computer. Such programs will meet the needs of a growing population: (1) students whose skills do not fit comfortably into any class level, (2) students (or faculty) who have taken formal coursework in the distant past and want to get back in touch with the language, and (3) students interested in studying a language for which no formal coursework is offered. The latter includes the less commonly taught languages, an increasingly vital resource in today's diversified society, yet one which is becoming more and more problematic for budget-strapped departments.

Finally, in studying ways of setting up or remodeling existing language labs, colleges should take a close look at how today's labs are being used.[3] Because video and computer material is now being more closely integrated into the classroom curriculum, many schools are modifying the traditional concept of the lab as sole audio-visual area in favor of installing two or three "media classrooms" and making the lab more of a resource center, a drop-in media library for both students and faculty. The media classroom would feature the equipment needed by the teacher for display: a VCR, a television monitor, a computer connected to a laserdisc player and/or CD-ROM or CD audio. The resource center (the former lab) should be equipped to attract browsers, with an ample collection of foreign language films on videotape and videodisc, CALL software keyed to classroom cur-

---

[3]The International Association of Language Laboratories (IALL) will provide free consulting to schools interested in remodeling or establishing a media center.

riculum, and both materials and personnel to support individualized instruction. It should be laid out so as to provide workstations for students working individually or in groups of two or three (situated along the walls in an irregular pattern), and an area in the center for larger group work, including viewing video together on a large-screen monitor.

In all of this, the department and the faculty must not lose sight of the humanitarian values which brought them to language study in the first place—and of the irreplaceable role of the warm and caring teacher.

BIBLIOGRAPHY

Altman, Rick. *The Video Connection: Integrating Video into Language Teaching.* Boston: Houghton Mifflin, 1989.

Association of Departments of Foreign Languages, Modern Language Association. "Language Learning and Hypermedia." *ADFL Bulletin*, 1988, Vol. 19, No. 3, pp. 13–17.

Borchardt, Frank L. "Press Any Key to Continue: Technology and Fantasy for the Rest of the 90's." *CALICO Journal*, 1991, Vol. 8, No. 4, pp. 17–24.

"Guidelines for Off-Air Recording of Broadcast Programming for Educational Purposes" Presented to Congress with additional comments, background information, and letters by Representative Robert W. Kastenmeier and recorded in the *Congressional Record*, October 14, 1981, pp. E4750–E4752.

Higgins, John and Tim Johns. *Computers in Language Learning.* Reading, Massachusetts: Addison-Wesley, 1984.

Higgins, John. "Problems of Self-Correction in the Language Laboratory." *System*, 1975, Vol. 3, No. 3, pp. 145–56.

Kramsch, Claire, Douglas Morgenstern, and Janet H. Murray. "An Overview of the MIT Athena Language Learning Project." *CALICO Journal*, 1985, Vol. 2, pp. 31–34.

Underwood, John. *Linguistics, Computers and the Language Teacher: A Communicative Approach.* Rowley, Massachusetts: Newbury House, 1984.

"On the Edge: Intelligent CALL in the 1990's." *Computers in the Humanities*, 1989, Vol. 23, pp. 71–84.

J OYCE S. T SUNODA

Foreign Language Instruction Across the Curriculum: A Strategy and Model

"The next step in the development of international studies is clearly one that requires some cross-course, cross-departmental, cross-school, cross-function innovation and coordination . . . Educational institutions need to go beyond the mastery of language skills and focus on the access that those language skills give to the particular knowledge and perspectives of other nations . . . for this information is directly applicable to the humanities, the social sciences . . . and to all the substantive realm of undergraduate education."

> Richard Lambert
> from *International Studies and the Undergraduate*

"Foreign language departments in many colleges have pointed the way for other humanities fields by emphasizing that knowledge of foreign languages has a growing vocational utility in today's world. Business, the professions, and the nature and character of work are centrally important aspects of contemporary culture, yet they receive relatively little attention from historians, philosophers, sociologists, anthropologists, and representatives of other humanities and social sciences disciplines."

> John W. Chandler
> from an address to the Association of American Colleges

INTRODUCTION

Foreign language instruction traditionally stressed rote memorization of common expressions, vocabulary, and sentence patterns as a primary technique for students to acquire skill in a new language. Cultural immersion within the classroom and proficiency-based

Joyce S. Tsunoda is Chancellor for Community Colleges and Senior Vice President at the University of Hawaii. Robert W. Franco, Robin Fujikawa, Louise Pagotto and Loretta Pang also contributed to this paper.

education which provided realistic experiences have also been popular instructional strategies. More recently, the application of educational technology to language learning has stimulated great enthusiasm. Many other innovative techniques have been successfully employed in language instruction.

Like any other skill, however, a foreign language is most easily acquired when the student has a vital interest and need to acquire the skill. Students are strongly motivated when proficiency in another language is relevant to their everyday experiences. This is best demonstrated by the apparent ease with which children assimilate languages because of their earnest interest in interacting with the world around them. Those who have had the opportunity to live in other countries also find themselves integrating new words, phrases, and sentences much more easily than in the classroom because of constant exposure to the language and to the culture.

An across-the-curriculum approach attempts to provide a natural environment which stimulates interest in learning a foreign language by providing opportunities to use the language and encouraging an understanding of the social, historical, and cultural context of the country of origin. The across-the-curriculum approach is a strategy to stimulate on campus the environment a student would normally encounter in a study abroad program. This approach enhances classroom instruction and provides the foundation for advance language study and study abroad experiences.

Interdisciplinary programs have been successfully established on many campuses. Kalamazoo Community College, MI is among the leaders in this area, offering both an Associate in Arts degree and a certificate in international education which incorporate language learning.

In contrast to an interdisciplinary approach, however, the across-the-curriculum strategy extends past traditional liberal arts boundaries to vocational education, providing vital linkages to the humanities and sciences for technical students who must be equally prepared for a new international environment.

In looking for models to improve foreign language instruction in the community colleges, we need to remember that despite the intrinsic intellectual value of learning other languages, the ultimate goal of foreign language instruction is to facilitate communication and understanding. Foreign language instruction is an avenue toward greater appreciation for human culture (the purview of the humanities), but it is also a vehicle to develop global perspectives and to promote the economic and social advancement of the individual. As the AACC Commission on the Future of Community Colleges points out, "In the century ahead, parochialism is not an option."[1] Language learning today must be viewed in the broader context of international studies and economic development. This paper describes ways to integrate foreign languages across-the-curriculum, particularly in the humanities, based on the successful experiences of several community colleges in Hawaii.

SETTING THE STAGE

International studies, including language instruction, is an integral part of the University of Hawaii (UH) Community Colleges' curriculum in support of the state's commitment to a leadership role in the Asia-Pacific region. The community college system's commitment to internationalizing education is reflected in several planning documents.

The overriding goal is to provide a curriculum that is relevant for students living in a multicultural international environment through diverse foreign language offerings, exchange opportunities for staff and students, vocational training opportunities for foreign students, leadership in consortia promoting international education, and exporting and sharing the teaching and training expertise of UH Community Colleges' faculty and staff across the Pacific and Asia.

KAPIOLANI ASIA-PACIFIC PROGRAM EMPHASES (KAPE)

In 1986, Kapiolani Community College, one of seven campuses in the University of Hawaii Community College system, identified four across-the-curriculum themes—writing, critical thinking, computing, and Asian-Pacific. The Asian-Pacific program was largely inspired by faculty who saw the importance of providing a curriculum focus on international education with a strong foreign language program at its core.

---

[1]Commission on the Future of Community Colleges. *Building Communities: A Vision for a New Century.* Washington, D.C.: American Association of Community Colleges, 1988, p. 32.

The college developed a strategic plan providing for "grassroots empowerment," that is, the locus of control was placed with faculty and staff who would be responsible for implementing the programs. Two week-long institutes in Summer, 1987 gave faculty and staff the opportunity to develop proposals to infuse the four themes into existing courses and new courses. The campus administrators assumed the role of program "angels" who garnered the necessary resources to implement the faculty's visions.

The humanities department played a leadership role in developing the Asian-Pacific across-the-curriculum program from its inception. The humanities department provided one of the two Asian-Pacific program coordinators (the other came from the social sciences department), who were given release time. The humanities department also played an important role in designing certificate programs for liberal arts students during the second summer institute and, further, provided an instructor to function as director of an international food fair and festival that has become a vital part of internationalizing the campus.

It Starts with Language Arts

Kapiolani's Asia-Pacific Program Emphases (KAPE) is rooted in a strong language arts department offering nine Asian-Pacific languages, some of which may be considered as the "lesser taught" languages, i.e., Samoan, Tagalog, and Mandarin. The college currently offers two years of instruction in all nine languages, with more than 25 percent of the student population enrolled in these courses.

Two distinct forces stimulated expansion of the diversity of foreign language offerings. In 1989, the University of Hawaii at Manoa added a second year of foreign language study to its requirements for the baccalaureate degree. Also, as KAPE gained momentum, funds from Title VI and the community college chancellor's office enabled Kapiolani to support a wider range of Asian and Pacific languages. First-year courses in Mandarin, Chinese, Samoan, and Tagalog were added to a curriculum which already had strong offerings in Japanese, Hawaiian, Spanish, and French. First semester courses in Korean and Russian were added respectively in Fall, 1989 and Fall, 1990.

The humanities faculty worked closely to ensure a good representation of global languages such as Mandarin and Russian, and local languages with limited usage, such as Samoan and Tagalog. French and Spanish were included as Asian-Pacific languages because of the continuing influence of French in New Caledonia and French Polynesia, and of Spanish in the Philippines and the Mariana Islands.

LANGUAGE INFUSION

A primary assumption in the Asian-Pacific across-the-curriculum program is that courses in related humanities, natural and social science disciplines, as well as vocational fields, should complement the foreign language program and vice versa. Therefore, new courses were introduced into the curriculum to specifically address this assumption.

Foreign language instruction is based on proficiency-based pedagogy, which presents realistic situations the student may encounter, such as ordering food in a restaurant. In addition to courses targeted for baccalaureate transfer, the language arts department developed industry-oriented courses to meet the practical needs of vocational education students and the local community. Basic conversational courses such as Japanese for the Visitor Industry, Mandarin, and Hawaiian provide proficiency in common expressions and "cultural cues" in everyday situations. Learning a simple phrase such as

Joyce Tsunoda addresses the AACC Foreign Language Education Roundtable. Also pictured: John Underwood and Elizabeth Welles, Program Officer, National Endowment for the Humanities.

"Doozo" (This way, please) in a basic Japanese class enabled a local security guard to save a group of 50 Japanese visitors during a hotel fire. A byproduct of KAPE has been the strengthening of the English as a Second Language (ESL) program by allowing non-English speaking students to tutor other students. The business education program actively encourages students to take advantage of the basic conversational courses. The sales and marketing division has recently developed a new course on international marketing, which demonstrates the role of cultural dynamics in foreign markets, as well as business customs and practices. Students in this course are encouraged to take higher level Asian-Pacific language courses to better appreciate the cultural environment in which they will be doing business.

FOREIGN LANGUAGES IN THE HUMANITIES

Beyond the development of new courses, language study has been incorporated into a wide variety of existing humanities, social sciences, and science courses. An excellent example of how the integration of language can enhance learning in the humanities is an Asian philosophy course which explicitly links language with culture. The course incorporates foreign terms as well as short excerpts from the works of foreign authors to demonstrate how cultural philosophies are reflected in language. For example, students are shown how the frequent absence of the personal pronoun in the Japanese language reflects Japan's predominant philosophies which diminish individual importance. In contrast, the first person in English is emphasized by capitalization and frequent placement at the beginning of a phrase.

How words are written is frequently as important as their meaning. A unit on Chinese philosophies concludes with a brief simulation of how calligraphy is learned in China and Japan. The students begin by cleaning the room and its surroundings and by cutting bamboo to fashion elementary brushes. They are then taught how to sit, breathe, and prepare mentally, as well as how to prepare the ink. When all is readied, with the teacher's hand as a guide and with intense concentration on what is to be written, the student executes a character in one breath. The exercise can be used to show, among other things, how Taoist spontaneity and Confucian discipline may be complementary in practice although conceptually contradictory.

Kapiolani students may also take a two-semester sequence of Asian history courses. In these courses, numerous examples of the historical and cultural role of language in the evolution of Asian civilizations are discussed. Until English became a powerful tool in British attempts to colonize and unify the region, linguistic diversity contributed to the fragmentation of South Asia for centuries. Indian languages strongly influenced Southeast Asian writing systems. In East Asia, the Chinese writing system played a unifying role in the cultural and intellectual traditions of China, Korea, and Japan, despite the significant differences which merged in the spoken languages of these three cultures. Through the Sanskrit and Pali texts, languages have also been a unifying factor in Buddhism across many Asian cultures.

In the social science department, anthropology courses explore the evolution of the human brain and the capacity for language. Cultural Anthropology investigates the relationship between language and perception in the cultures of India, Thailand, Indonesia, Samoa, ancient Hawaii, and New Zealand. Nursing students who are required to take this course are sensitized to cultural differences in both verbal and non-verbal communication. Pacific Islands Peoples explores issues of European colonizing and language loss and bilingual/bicultural issues in contemporary Pacific Islands education, particularly as they related to accelerating patterns of out-migration. Other social sciences courses, such as political science, American studies, and geography, are infused with substantial Asian-Pacific content.

In the natural sciences, ethnobotany introduces students to the scientific and indigenous names of Asian and Pacific plants, and their cultural significance. Botanical evidence of plant origins in Asia supports Austronesian linguistic evidence for the human settlement of the Pacific Islands. Hawaiian botany and zoology courses also convey both the scientific and indigenous names of flora and fauna, and their use in Hawaii's broader cultural context.

All of these activities encourage an appreciation for other languages and cultures. Students also learn foreign terminology for specific fields.

STUDY ABROAD OPPORTUNITIES

Interdisciplinary programs have been introduced on various scales at the other Hawaii community colleges. Each campus has a strong relationship with a sister school in Japan or another country, offering field experiences and humanities and language instruction. Leeward Community College on the island of Oahu offered a three-week intensive study tour of Japan in 1986. In the late 1980s, Leeward added a series of three-credit courses on Japanese culture taught by visiting Beppu University professors to its summer school curriculum. Beppu University (whose president is a noted artist in Japan) is a private four-year campus with a strong humanities program. The first two courses in this series were Japanese Culture from the Perspective of the Japanese Farmer, and Modern Japanese Literature. A third course on Japanese calligraphy was well-received by both on-campus students and the community. All of the courses were taught through local translators. The series continues to be offered in odd numbered years.

Windward Community College has a sister college relationship with Kagawa College in Japan. This relationship provides for reciprocal student exchanges each year, and as part of the Summer, 1991 program, Kagawa and Windward faculty artists exchanged their respective art work for public exhibitions in Japan and in Hawaii. It was the first Japan-U.S. art exhibit exchange involving a two-year college.

Seven Kapiolani students studied Chinese language and literature at the Central Institute of Nationalities, Beijing, lead by a Kapiolani instructor of Mandarin during Summer, 1991.

CREATING A CAMPUS ENVIRONMENT

Kapiolani's administration, staff, and faculty have also enthusiastically promoted activities that encourage linguistic and cultural expression. These include ethnic clubs such as the Pacific Asian Student Association, and Korean, Japanese, Chinese, Filipino-American, and Samoan clubs and a campus lecture series which has featured a noted Confucianist scholar, experts on East Asian kanji (script) and South Asian dowry, and specialists on Hawaiian chant and Polynesian oratory.

Each spring the campus sponsors an international festival, featuring ethnic foods, lecturers, forums, cultural performances, and Asian-Pacific films, all of which stimulate thematic discussions. The festivals are organized around such themes as "Life Forces: East and West." The themes provide the KAPE committee with a broad interpretive framework for the inclusion of many diverse multicultural activities. Over the years, students have been able to observe a Samoan kava ceremony performed in the high chiefly language, diverse forms of

Hawaiian, Muslim and Buddhist chant, East and Southeast Asian dance performances with songs in indigenous languages, and Samoan, Marshallese, Pohnpeian, and Chuukese choral performances, also in indigenous languages. The performances are usually held in the campus cafeteria where students experience the cuisine of the culture represented.

An international student conference provides students with a forum to explore and express meaningful concepts from Asian and Pacific languages. Last year, award-winning papers explored the Chinese concepts of conflict and spiritual growth, and the south Asian notions of life cycle and spiritual growth. In previous years, students have discussed Polynesian concepts of mana and tabu and Confucianist notions of the role of the individual in society.

Faculty and students are further exposed to Asian-Pacific and international language and culture at the annual Hawaii International Film Festival. These films showcase the talents of indigenous Asian and Pacific region filmmakers. One final strategy needs to be mentioned in creating a campus environment conducive to foreign language learning. Many Kapiolani administrators and faculty spend their summer months and sabbatical leaves in Asia and the Pacific region. When they return to the campus, they often have students in their classrooms with linguistic and cultural ties to the regions they visited. Frequently one can hear faculty greet students in their native languages and then discuss contemporary events in their homelands. Similarly, after students return from a visit home, they update the faculty member on current developments. These interpersonal interactions leave powerful impressions on both the faculty and the student, impressing each with the compelling power of language as a vehicle for friendship and collegiality.

THE PROCESS

As mentioned earlier, administrative support has been very strong. However, the faculty has been responsible for program development and control from the outset.

Like many community colleges, Kapiolani's campus-based system of tenure and promotion facilitates cross-curricula cooperation. Unlike the department-driven reward system common to many universities, Kapiolani's faculty can venture across departmental lines without fear of neglecting the locus of the reward system. Kapiolani's success is partly due to the administration's taking advantage of the interdisciplinary reward system, trusting the faculty's ability to work cooperatively in an across-the-curriculum effort and to be responsible for KAPE.

Administrative support and faculty direction were both key factors in the two summer institutes held in 1987 and 1988. At these institutes, faculty members from both liberal arts and vocational areas met to discuss how they could infuse Asian Pacific cultures and languages into their courses. Each participant submitted a proposal for a project to be implemented the following semester. Among the proposed project titles were "Myth and Meditation in Asian and Western Religions," "Music Cultures of Asia and the Pacific," "Asian and Pacific Marketing," and "Cultural Factors in Health Care."

The summer institutes did more than change the curriculum. From these institutes faculty members developed a profound respect for the Asian and Pacific instructional expertise on campus. This is reflected in the more than 50 faculty members on campus who are involved in KAPE. New faculty with Asian-Pacific expertise enter a teaching environment which encourages further scholarly development and provides fresh intellectual energy to the program.

One result is increasing curricular coherence. With the creation of new foreign language courses, new courses dedicated to Asia and the Pacific, and ongoing curricular infusion, Kapiolani has international courses in all four liberal arts departments. Students are able to enter an Asian and Pacific track leading to an Associate in Arts degree, and transfer credits to Hawaiian, Asian, or Pacific Studies, and other departments at the four-year campus. Students in business, nursing and allied health, food service and hotel operations not only have a wide range of Asian and Pacific courses supporting their general education, but a wide range of specifically designed courses enhancing their understanding of Asia, the Pacific, and Hawaii.

CONCLUSION

Development of parallel activities across-the-curriculum and across-the-campus can reinforce and energize the language instruction program at community colleges. The perception of language as a "window" to cross-cultural appreciation as well as a communications tool can be encouraged to support language learning. Co-curricular activities also reinforce curricular offerings and classroom instruction.

BETTE G. HIRSCH AND CHANTAL P. THOMPSON

Proficiency Goals and the Teaching of Literature in the Foreign Language Classroom

SOME DATE THE BEGINNINGS OF THE PROFICIENCY MOVEMENT TO 1979, when the report of the President's Commission on Foreign Language and International Studies described Americans' foreign language incompetence as "nothing short of scandalous." The Commission recommended that national attention be focused on the development of the foreign language proficiency of U.S. students.

The United States government, long concerned with producing students at its many language schools who could *use* language, not just analyze it, had already created a scale for measuring the language proficiency of all—from the beginner to the equivalent of the well-educated native speaker. The scale measured proficiency in four skill areas: reading, writing, listening, and speaking. Tests existed for each area, most notably an oral proficiency test to measure speaking ability.

In the early 1980's, the American Council on the Teaching of Foreign Languages (ACTFL), in conjunction with the Educational Testing Service (ETS), adapted this government model to suit the needs of academic programs. The following chart (p. 62) of Assessment Criteria: Speaking Proficiency introduces elements of the ACTFL scale.

In 1982, a small group of language instructors began introducing colleagues to the ACTFL proficiency scale, the techniques of oral proficiency testing, and their applications to the classroom. Since then, many instructors have changed the ways and means by which they teach languages, new proficiency-based textbooks have been created, and an excellent proficiency-based methods book, *Teaching*

Bette G. Hirsch is Division Chair of Foreign Languages and Communications at Cabrillo College, CA.

Chantal P. Thompson is a Lecturer in French at Brigham Young University.

ASSESSMENT CRITERIA: SPEAKING PROFICIENCY

GLOBAL TASKS/FUNCTIONS	CONTEXT	CONTEXT	ACCURACY	TEXT TYPE
Superior Can discuss extensively by supporting opinions, abstracting and hypothesizing	Most formal and informal settings	Wide range of general interest topics and some special fields of interest and expertise; concrete, abstract and unfamiliar topics	Errors virtually never interfere with communication or disturb the native speaker	Extended discourse
Advanced Can describe and narrate in major time/aspect frames	Most informal and some formal settings	Concrete and factual topics of personal and public interest	Can be understood without difficulty and speakers unaccustomed to non-native speakers	Paragraph discourse
Intermediate Can maintain simple face-to-face conversation by asking and responding to simple questions	Some informal settings and a limited number of transactional situations	Topics related primarily to self and immediate environment	Can be understood, with some repetition, by speakers accustomed to non-native speakers	Discrete sentences and strings of sentences
Novice Can produce only formulaic utterances, lists and enumerations	Highly predictable daily settings	Common discrete elements of daily life	May be difficult to understand, even for those accustomed to non-native speakers	Discrete words and phrases

Reprinted with permission, American Council on the Teaching of Foreign Languages (ACTFL).

Language In Context, has been written by Alice Omaggio. Hundreds of two-year college instructors (as well as those at universities and in high schools) have attended familiarization workshops to introduce them to proficiency principles, and a significant number of two-year institutions have shifted the emphasis of their programs toward proficiency.

This paper will examine major characteristics of proficiency-oriented foreign language classes as they exist currently at two-year colleges. It will further explore the role of literature in these classes: how the principles of the proficiency-oriented classroom can make fine literature accessible to the intermediate-level student, and how the reading of this literature can then lead to the development of speaking and writing proficiency. Our emphasis here is how literature can be part of the intermediate foreign language curriculum, but we feel strongly that literature can and should be introduced to students during their first year of language study.

THE PROFICIENCY-ORIENTED CLASSROOM

Proficiency-oriented classes do not have book chapters and structural points to be "covered" as objectives, but rather, they stress what students can *do* with language. Indeed, as Donald Rice states, "The fundamental notion of the proficiency movement is that of *doing*, the idea that it is what we want students to be able to *do* that should determine what they need to know." (p. 13) In some cases, proficiency-oriented classes represent individual efforts, and in others, language departments have made this commitment.

These classes look at each of the four skills (reading, writing, listening, speaking) separately, knowing that students are likely to develop proficiency in each skill with varied rapidity. For example, a second-year college student is likely to have higher listening and reading proficiency than speaking and writing proficiency. Instructors in proficiency-oriented classes choose materials and activities that will specifically strengthen the current proficiency of students and help them move on to the next level.

Instructors with a proficiency orientation often identify and work with four proficiency levels for each skill: Novice, Intermediate, Advanced, and Superior. These terms, from the ACTFL scale (see the preceding chart on Assessment Criteria), detail what tasks students can accomplish with language, in what contexts, and with what accuracy. Learner proficiency progresses through the following levels:

Novice: Students function using isolated words, such as found in lists and charts. They often speak and write in sentence fragments, recycling textbook material and adding words in English. Most student skills in the first year course are at this level.

Intermediate: Students function by creating sentences, putting together what they have learned in a new way to talk about themselves and others. They ask and answer questions and can navigate through every-day situations. Most students in proficiency- oriented classes can attain this level in their skills during their second year of study.

Advanced: Students are able to speak and write in paragraphs. They can narrate and describe in past, present and future times and generally talk about the world. They can handle complicated situations and make themselves understood by any native speaker. Although reading and listening proficiency may be at this level by the end of the second year of foreign language study, studies have shown that it is only at the end of four years of study that most students can speak and write at this level.

Superior: Students function using extended discourse. They are fully professional and can talk about ideas and the abstract realm. Their errors rarely disturb the native speaker. Students usually reach this level during graduate studies and after an extended period of time living and studying in a country where the language is spoken.

Proficiency-oriented classes use authentic materials that present real language in real contexts. Literature can be perfect for this. It asks important questions. It can complement other authentic materials (timetables, menus, advertisements, magazine and newspaper articles) to increase students' comprehension of the culture being studied. It is very different from the passages created for textbooks! These pas-sages, unfortunately, often sound like, to paraphrase Ionesco in *The Bald Soprano* as he mocks typical textbook language, "Today is Tuesday. It comes before Wednesday and after Monday!"

Proficiency-oriented classes are not run by any one method, but select presen-tation/practice strategies that involve students in mean-ingful practice and help them stretch up to the next higher proficiency level in each skill. This real-life practice can lead to skills integration (improvement across the skills). Some techniques of practice include:

—Real language that is used in context and to perform real functions.

—Many paired and small-group activities—perfect for sharing reader reaction.

—Topics and functions that are recycled to allow development.

—Personalization of material.

—Activities that have a purpose—an information gap to be closed.

One goal of this type of proficiency-oriented class is to develop students' reading skills. The question for us is "How does literature fit in?" Our aim is to show how the techniques mentioned above, when used in the proficiency-based "class," can make it possible for the intermediate student to read literature. If we wait for the student to be truly advanced before introducing literature, in a third year language course for example, we have lost at least 90% of all students. This is not acceptable.

PREPARATION FOR READING LITERATURE

Whatever level of difficulty, proper pre-reading preparation can yield access for intermediate students. As stated by Joanne Collie and Stephen Slater in *Literature in the Language Classroom*, these pre-reading activities can convince students "that the task ahead is not an impossible one." (p. 16) They will succeed, and as C.J. Brumfit and R.A. Carter in *Literature and Language Teaching* suggest, we can, perhaps, prevent students from disliking a text because it contains some literary convention that they do not understand or very difficult language. (p. 23) They also add that we are "socializing students into a community of serious readers." (p. 31)

What kind of activities are useful? We have selected six—one per century or period of time—as examples. The passages, presented on the following pages, are in French, but our focus here is on the pre-reading or *preparation* work, which is in English. These pages are extracted from *Moments Littéraires*, an intermediate-level college text by Hirsch and Thompson.

Activity 1—Middle Ages: Charles d'Orléans, "Le Printemps" (Personification)

Activity 2—16th Century: Montaigne, *De l'amitié* (Skim for the main idea)

Activity 3—17th Century: Molière, *L'Ecole des Femmes*
(Brainstorming)
Activity 4—18th Century: Montesquieu, *Lettres Persanes* (Point
of view)
Activity 5—19th Century: George Sand, *François le champi*
(Skim for character traits)
Activity 6—20th Century: Marguerite Duras, *La Pluie d'été*
(Characterization)

In each activity, you will see that the pre-reading serves to engage students actively in the reading process. The demanded task necessitates the production of words and of lists, not paragraphs or extended discourse, as has been the case in the past in many non-proficiency-oriented textbooks. These short responses are within the capability of intermediate-level students who can often read at a much more sophisticated level than they can write or speak. They must extract meaning from the known and unknown words in order to be able to accomplish the task within the given time frame. This fast read through, or other preparation, often helps avoid the futile dictionary search to translate every word that defeats so many readers. The six activities we have selected as examples are on pages 68–79.

EXPLORING THE CREATIVE DIMENSION OF LANGUAGE THROUGH LITERATURE

Whether we use it to teach language, culture, or literature in its own right, literature's beauty is that it provides authentic texts that engage the reader beyond sheer comprehension.

On the linguistic side, "Literature provides a rich context in which individual lexical or syntactical items are made more memorable . . . Literary language is sometimes elaborate, sometimes marvelously simple yet, somehow, absolutely 'right' . . . Figurative language [casts] new light on familiar sensations and [opens] up new dimensions of perception in a way that can be exhilarating but also startling and even unsettling." If the texts are well chosen and made accessible through proper pre-reading, students can "begin to appreciate the richness and variety of the language they are trying to master" and they can become more creative and adventurous themselves in the language. (Collie and Slater, p. 5)

As Peter Schofer points out in his excellent article, "Literature and Communicative Competence," that literary devices such as metaphors, comparisons and metonymies, which actually "permeate every part of our lives," give a new dimension to language, even a foreign language. "Through intimate contact with the authentic text as a model,. . . students learn *how* different types of language actually function." Thus, "It can be said not only that literature is in the land of language, but that the literary is an integral part of our world of language instruction." (*FL Annals*, pp. 332–3)

In *Moments Littéraires*, students learn to identify and appreciate various literary devices. One example mentioned earlier is personification. In the pre-reading for "Le Printemps" by Charles d'Orléans, students are asked to focus on personification. In the post-reading, they are asked to react to those personifications and create some of their own:

"Quel est l'effet de la personnification du temps sur vous en tant que lecteur/lectrice? Quelles autres personnifications vous viennent à l'esprit quand vous pensez au temps et aux saisons?"

["How does the personification of time affect you as a reader? What other personifications come to your mind as you think about time and seasons?"]

With famous authors as models, students create their own similes, metaphors, symbols, antitheses and personifications; involved in the creative process, they forget their inhibitions and truly "create with the language." By exploring the *creative* dimension of language, students come dramatically closer to making the foreign language their own. The following activity serves as an illustration.

Consider a third semester French class during the first week of school. The function being worked on is description of self and others in the present. Adjectives are needed to perform this function. While working on adjectives, the teacher introduces "Rouge," a song by contemporary French singer and poet Michel Sardou, about an adjective and all the comparisons that this adjective evokes:

"Rouge, comme un soleil couchant de Méditerranée
Rouge, comme les joues d'un enfant quand il a trop joué
Rouge, comme la pomme qui te donne le parfum du péché
Rouge, comme le feu d'un volcan qui va se réveiller"

ACTIVITY 1: Middle Ages

✦ *"Le Printemps,"* by *Charles d'Orléans*

PREPARATION

A. Etude de mots

Though old French spelling (**le vieux français**) differs from modern French, many changes are readily recognizable. An **s** between a vowel and a consonant, for example, is often dropped in modern French and replaced by a circumflex over the vowel, as in **hospital/hôpital**, or **vestir/vêtir (habiller)**. The letter **y** in old French has often become an **i**, as in **pluye/pluie**. Letters have been added in some cases, and deleted in others.

See if you can deduce the modern French equivalents for the words below that appear in the poem. If all else fails, you may find it helpful to pronounce troublesome words aloud.

laissié	s'abille	beste	oyseau
cler	souleil	chascun	

B. La Personnification

You will at times be able to identify in a poem an image around which the poem is constructed, such as **le temps** in this rondeau. The treatment of **le temps** as a person is called **personnification,** a literary device you will often encounter.

As you read the poem a first time, list the verbs and nouns that personify **le temps.**

✦ LE PRINTEMPS

Le temps a laissié son manteau
De vent, de froidure et de pluye,
Et s'est vestu de broderie
De souleil luyant,° cler et beau.   luisant, brillant

5   Il n'y a beste ne° oyseau   ni
Qu'°en son jargon ne chante ou crie: Qui
«Le Temps a laissié son manteau
De vent, de froidure et de pluye.»

Rivière, fontaine et ruisseau°   petite rivière
10   Portent en livrée° jolie   costume
Gouttes° d'argent d'orfavrerie;°   *drops* / travaillées par
Chascun s'abille de nouveau.   un artisan

Le temps a laissié son manteau
De vent, de froidure et de pluye,
15   Et s'est vestu de broderie
De souleil luyant, cler et beau.

—*Rondeau VI,* 15° siècle

69

ACTIVITY 2:   16th Century

✦ *"De l'amitié,"* by *Montaigne*

PREPARATION

An essay is a short composition on a single subject, usually presenting the personal views of the author. As you read for the first time the passage that follows, note in the margins of your book the main idea of each paragraph of the essay. During subsequent readings, and in the comprehension work after the reading, you will be able to look back at these initial notes and examine more closely how Montaigne manages to present his ideas about friendship.

✦ DE L'AMITIÉ

Ce que nous appelons ordinairement amis et amitiés,
ce ne sont qu'accointances et familiarités nouées° par   formées
quelque occasion ou commodité, par le moyen de   restent ensemble
laquelle nos âmes s'entretiennent.° En l'amitié dont
5 je parle, elles se mêlent et se confondent° l'une en   se mêlent... *mix and*
l'autre, d'un mélange si universel qu'elles effacent° et   *blend* / font disparaî-
ne retrouvent plus la couture° qui les a jointes. Si on   tre / *seam*
me presse de dire pourquoi je l'aimais je sens que
cela ne peut s'exprimer qu'en répondant: «Parce que
10 c'était lui, parce que c'était moi».

Il y a, au delà° de tout ce que je puis° en dire, je ne   en supplément / peux
sais quelle force inexplicable et fatale, médiatrice° de   à la base
cette union. Nous nous cherchions avant de nous être
vus, rapprochés° par des rapports que nous entendi-   *brought closer*
15 ons l'un de l'autre, et aussi, je crois, par quelque
ordonnance du ciel.° Nous nous embrassions° par   ordonnance... volonté
nos noms; et à notre première rencontre, qui fut par   de Dieu / étions unis
hasard en une grande fête et compagnie de ville, nous
nous trouvâmes si pris, si connus, si liés° entre nous,   attachés
20 que rien dès lors ne nous fut si proche que l'un à
l'autre. . . .

Qu'on ne mette pas en ce rang° ces autres amitiés   ce... cette catégorie
communes: j'en ai autant de connaissance qu'un
autre, mais je ne conseille pas qu'on confonde leurs
25 règles. Les autres amitiés, dans lesquelles il faut
marcher avec prudence et précaution, se nourrissent°   subsistent à cause
de services rendus et de bienfaits.° Mais en ce noble   faveurs / ce noble... la
commerce,° l'union de tels amis étant véritablement   vraie amitié
parfaite, elle leur fait perdre le sentiment de tels
30 devoirs, et chasser d'entre eux ces mots de division et
de différence: «bienfait, obligation, reconnaissance,°   gratitude
prière, remerciement», et leurs pareils.

ACTIVITY 3:   17th Century

✦ *"L'Ecole des femmes,"* by *Molière*

PREPARATION

Reading in a foreign language involves confronting both the known and the unknown. Brainstroming about possible directions in which a topic may develop prior to reading a passage about that topic can often help.

In the scenes you will read from Molière's *l'Ecole des femmes,* the discussion is about marriage and the ideal wife. Before you read these lines, your class will divide into three groups. One group will generate (in French if possible) a list of characteristics of the ideal wife that a traditional and very conservative man might propose. The second group will create a similar list for the wife of the "liberated male" of the 1990s. The third group will list what kind of woman a reasonable, "average" man might choose today. One member from each group will write the group's list on the board or on an overhead transparency and the class as a whole will compare the three lists. Then as you begin your first reading of the passage from *L'Ecole des femmes,* think about the characteristics of the ideal wife Molière chose to list in the play.

✦ L'Ecole des femmes

ACTE III, SCENE II

ARNOLPHE, AGNES

ARNOLPHE *(assis):* Agnès, pour m'écouter, laissez
    là votre ouvrage.°   travail
    Levez un peu la tête et tournez le visage:
    Là, regardez-moi là durant cet entretien,°   cette conversation
    Et jusqu'au moindre° mot imprimez-le-vous° bien.   plus petit / **impri-
                                             mez.** . . écoutez-le
5 Je vous épouse, Agnès; et cent fois la journée
    Vous devez bénir° l'heur de votre destinée,°   *bless* / (mot apparenté)
    Contempler la bassesse° où vous avez été,   misère
    Et dans le même temps admirer ma bonté,
    Qui de ce vil° état de pauvre villageoise   abject
10 Vous fait monter au rang° d'honorable bourgeoise **au.** . . à la condition
                                            sociale / **jouir.** . . bé-
    Et jouir de la couche° et des embrassements   néficier du lit / fuir
    D'un homme qui fuyait° tous ces engagements,   = *to flee*
    Et dont à vingt partis,° fort capables de plaire, personnes à marier
    Le coeur a refusé l'honneur qu'il vous veut faire.
15 Vous devez toujours, dis-je, avoir devant les yeux
    Le peu que vous étiez sans ce noeud° glorieux,   mariage
    Afin que cet objet° d'autant mieux vous instruise ici: cette idée

73

ACTIVITY 4:   18th Century

✦ *"Lettres persanes,"* by *Montesquieu*

PREPARATION

The *Lettres persanes* is actually a novel in the form of letters in which two Persians traveling in France, Rica and Usbek, write home and to one another, commenting on what they see and contrasting life in France with the customs in their native land. They also receive letters from home, keeping them informed about their affairs and reacting to the information in their letters.

When you read a passage, either fiction or nonfiction, in which the narrator's point of view may color the telling of a story, you as reader will want to place in perspective what is said. And in a subsequent reading you may want to question how the specific point of view has influenced the narrator's way of conveying certain details.

Clearly, the point of view of Rica and Usbek, as foreigners, shapes the manner in which they interpret what might seem very ordinary to a Frenchman of the time. This shift in viewpoint allows Montesquieu to examine the customs of his countrymen with a critical eye. As you read each letter a first time, list a few habits or characteristics of the French that strike the visitors as bizarre. Compare notes with classmates and be ready to draw upon your lists for postreading work.

✦ Lettres Persanes

LETTRE 24. RICA A IBBEN

Nous sommes à Paris depuis un mois, et nous avons
toujours été dans un mouvement continuel. Il faut
bien des affaires avant qu'on soit logé, qu'on ait
trouvé les gens à qui on est adressé, et qu'on se soit
5   pourvu des° choses nécessaires, qui manquent toutes   se... ait obtenu les
à la fois.

Paris est aussi grand qu'Ispahan:° les maisons y   ancienne capitale de la
sont si hautes qu'on jurerait qu'elles ne sont habitées   Perse
que par des astrologues. Tu juges bien qu'une ville
10   bâtie en l'air, qui a six ou sept maisons les unes sur
les autres, est extrêmement peuplée; et que, quand
tout le monde est descendu dans la rue, il s'y fait un
bel embarras.°   encombrement

Tu ne le croirais pas peut-être: depuis un mois que
15   je suis ici, je n'y ai encore vu marcher personne. Il n'y
a point de gens au monde qui tirent mieux parti de
leur machine° que les Français: ils courent, ils volent;   tirent... savent mieux
les voitures lentes d'Asie, le pas réglé de nos cha-   exploiter le corps
meaux,° les feraient tomber en syncope.° Pour moi,   humain / camels /
20   qui ne suis point fait à ce train,° et qui vais souvent   tomber... faint / fait...
à pied sans changer d'allure,° j'enrage quelquefois   habitué à ce rythme /
comme un chrétien: car encore passe° qu'on m'écla-   de façon de
bousse° depuis les pieds jusqu'à la tête; mais je ne puis   marcher / encore...
pardonner les coups de coude que je reçois régulière-   j'accepte / splash
25   ment et périodiquement. Un homme qui vient après
moi et qui me passe me fait faire un demi-tour; et un
autre qui me croise de l'autre côté me remet soudain
où le premier m'avait pris; et je n'ai pas fait cent pas,
que je suis plus brisé° que si j'avais fait dix lieues.°   fatigué / une lieue =
30   Ne crois pas que je puisse, quant à présent, te parler   4 km / à... de façon
à fond° des moeurs° et des coutumes européennes: je   complète / syn. de
n'en ai moi-même qu'une légère idée, et je n'ai eu à   coutumes
peine que le temps de m'étonner.

Le roi de France est le plus puissant° prince de   grand
35   l'Europe. Il n'a point de mines d'or comme le roi
d'Espagne son voisin; mais il a plus de richesses que
lui, parce qu'il les tire° de la vanité de ses sujets, plus   obtient
inépuisable° que les mines. On lui a vu entreprendre   endless
ou soutenir de grandes guerres, n'ayant d'autres   ressources
40   fonds° que des titres d'honneur à vendre; et, par un
prodige de l'orgueil humain, ses troupes se trouvaient
payées, ses places munies,° et ses flottes équipées.   armées

75

ACTIVITY 5: 19th Century

✦ *"François le Champi,"*
by George Sand

PREPARATION

This novel by George Sand presents eleven years in the life of François le Champi. "Champi" is defined by Sand as "l'enfant abandonné dans les champs". We meet Madeleine Blanchet and her family and see how their life in a small village changes once François arrives there.

   In Chapter 1 of the novel, which follows, you will learn a lot about François. It is often useful in a first reading to identify characteristics of a central figure. As you read here, underline passages that give you these details and then complete the following chart.

Traits physiques	*Traits de personnalité*
1.	1.
2.	2.
3.	3.
4.	4.
etc.	

✦ FRANÇOIS LE CHAMPI [extrait]

Un matin que Madeleine Blanchet, la jeune meunière du Cormouer, s'en allait au bout de son pré pour laver à la fontaine, elle trouva un petit enfant assis devant sa planchette, et jouant avec la paille qui sett
5 de coussinet aux genoux des lavandières. Madeleine Blanchet, ayant avisé cet enfant, fut étonnée de ne pas le connaître, car il n'y a pas de route bien achalandée de passants de ce côté-là, et on n'y rencontre que des gens de l'endroit.
10 —Qui es-tu, mon enfant? dit-elle au petit garçon, qui la regardait d'un air de confiance, mais qui ne parut pas comprendre sa question. Comment t'appelles-tu? reprit Madeleine Blanchet en le faisant asseoir à côté d'elle et en s'agenouillant pour laver.
15 —François, répondit l'enfant.
—François qui?
—Qui? dit l'enfant d'un air simple.
—A qui es-tu fils?
—Je ne sais pas, allez!
—Tu ne sais pas le nom de ton père!
—Je n'en ai pas.
—Il est donc mort?

miller / petit village du Berry (au centre de la France) / *wash board* / *straw* / petit coussin / femmes qui lavent le linge / vu

fréquentée

ACTIVITY 6: 20th Century

✦ *"La Pluie d'été,"* by Marguerile Duras

PREPARATION

Marguerite Duras, in this novel published in 1990, paints the portrait of an unusual family that lives on the fringes of society in Vitry, outside of Paris. Their seven children do not attend school, yet books and reading play an important role in their lives. As you read, underline the beginning of each mention of this interest in books. Then make a chart similar to the following one noting relevant facts about each family member's link with reading and books.

Membres de la famille	Rôle des livres
le père	
la mère	
Ernesto	
Jeanne	
les jeunes brothers et sisters	

✦ La Pluie d'été [extrait]

Les livres, le père les trouvait dans les trains de ban-
lieue. Il les trouvait aussi séparés des poubelles, *à côté*
comme offerts, après les décès ou les déménagements. *président de la Ré-*
Une fois il avait trouvé *La Vie de Georges Pompidou.* *publique française*
5 Par deux fois il avait lu ce livre-là. Il y avait aussi des *(1969–1974) / assem-*
vieilles publications techniques ficelées en paquets *blées*
près des poubelles ordinaires mais ça, il laissait. La
mère aussi avait lu *La Vie de Georges Pompidou.*
Cette *Vie* les avait également passionnés. Après celle-
10 là ils avaient recherché des *Vies...*

["Red, like a setting sun on the Mediterranean Sea
Red, like the cheeks of a child who has played too much
Red, like the apple that gives you the aroma of sin
Red, like the fire of a volcano about to wake up"]

After a listening activity to discover the model, students are asked to choose an adjective and, in groups of two or three, create as many comparisons as they can in eight minutes. They love it. When the eight minutes are up, they do not want to stop. They speak, they write, they feel, they create in French. The excitement is complete when the teacher "prints" their poems and distributes them to the class as their first "publication" in French. Here are a few samples of such creations by second-year students in their first week of school.

Triste	Sad
Triste, comme un enfant perdu	Sad, like a lost child
Triste, comme le ciel quand il pleut	Sad, like the sky when it rains
Triste, comme un vieil homme seul dans le parc	Sad, like an old man alone in the park
Triste, comme le dernier baiser à son père	Sad, like the last kiss to one's father
Triste, comme quelqu'un qui a perdu la vérité	Sad, like someone who has lost the truth.

Naïf	Naive
Naïf, comme la neige fraîche sur les montagnes	Naive, like fresh snow on the mountains
Naïf, comme le soleil du petit matin	Naive, like the early morning sun
Naïf, comme le nouveau-né	Naive, like the newborn child
Naïf, comme un monde sans guerre	Naive, like a world without war
Naïf, comme. . .nous.	Naive, like. . .us.

Indeed, literature—and some songs are literature—is an inspiring model. And why is it so helpful in the language learning process? Because it fosters personal involvement. To quote Collie and Slater again, "Engaging imaginatively with literature enables learners to shift the focus of their attention beyond the more mechanical aspects of the foreign language system." (p. 5)

With literature, there is some special incentive involved: "Enjoyment; suspense; a fresh insight into issues which are felt to be close to the heart of people's concerns; the delight of encountering one's own thoughts or situations encapsulated vividly in a work of art; the other, equal delight of finding those same thoughts or situations illuminated by a totally new, unexpected light or perspective: all these are incentives which can lead learners to overcome enthusiastically the linguistic obstacles that might be considered too great in less involving material." (Collie and Slater, pp. 6–7)

As Brumfit and Carter state in *Literature and Language Teaching,* "It will be a long time before a more versatile piece of educational technology than the paperback book is invented, and there is no more easily available source for personal growth than literature." (p. 34)

This growth, both linguistic and personal, is not likely to occur in the teacher-centered classroom where personal student investment is minimal. In the student-centered, or proficiency-oriented classroom, however, the possibilities for growth are endless.

LITERATURE AS A SPRINGBOARD FOR SPEAKING ACTIVITIES

Open-ended questions

What makes a good open-ended question, especially for intermediate-level students? In terms of proficiency, the contexts and content areas in which the intermediate-level speaker operates best are autobiographical or personal. Therefore, personalization is the key. Through personalization, the abstract ceases to be abstract. Through personalization, a transition is made between the world of ideas and the "me" world of the intermediate-level speaker. Let us consider some examples of seemingly difficult open-ended questions that intermediate-level students *can* handle and love to discuss—because they are personalized. Note that most of these open-ended question activities are conducted in small groups to maximize participation and minimize anxiety. The examples are taken from *Moments Littéraires.*

Question on Montaigne's essay, "De l'amitié":

La phrase de Montaigne "parce que c'était lui, parce que c'était moi" a été reprise par de nombreux artistes, en particulier dans le monde de la chanson. Parlez d'une expérience que vous avez partagée avec quelqu'un, "parce que c'était lui (ou elle), parce que c'était moi."

[Montaigne's phrase "Because it was he, because it was I" has been used by many artists, especially in songs. Tell about an experience that you have shared with someone, "because it was he/she, because it was you."]

Question on Victor Hugo's poem, "Demain d XC47,1 s l'aube. . .":

Pour se rapprocher de sa fille, Victor Hugo se sépare du monde extérieur. Le souvenir, en tant que réalité intérieure, est-il toujours incompatible avec le monde extérieur? Donnez des illustrations personnelles. Dans quelles circonstances vous arrive-t-il de ne pas faire attention au monde extérieur? Donnez plusieurs exemples.

[To get closer to the memory of his deceased daughter, Victor Hugo separates himself from the outside world. Is memory, as an inside reality, always incompatible with the outside world? Give some personal illustrations. In what circumstances do you exclude or ignore the outside world? Give several examples.]

Questions on Cyrano's famous "nose" monologue:

1. On dit que la meilleure défense est une bonne offensive. Cyrano a un nez qui le défigure. Avant que les autres ne puissent le critiquer, il se décrit d'une manière spirituelle et amusante qui arrête les critiques des autres. C'est une des techniques utilisées par des gens qui ont peur d'être critiqués. Que pensez-vous de cette technique? Est-ce que vous avez jamais utilisé une telle technique? Donnez des exemples personnels.

[It is said that the best defense is a good offense. Cyrano has a nose that disfigures him. Before others can criticize him, he describes himself in a witty and amusing way that stops the criticisms of others. That is one technique used by people who are afraid of being criticized. What do you think of this technique? Have you ever used it? Give personal examples.]

2. Les exagérations dans la vie quotidienne:
a) Trouvez dans le texte les exemples d'exagérations qui vous frappent le plus. Expliquez pourquoi ce sont des exagérations.
b) Pensez aux exagérations que vous faites ou que vous entendez dans votre vie quotidienne. Faites une liste ensemble de ces exagérations.
c) Pour quelles raisons fait-on des exagérations?

[Exaggerations in daily life:
a) Find in the text examples of exaggerations; explain why they are so.
b) Make a list of exaggerations that you use or hear in your daily life.
c) Why do we exaggerate?]

Question on "La cantatrice chauve," by Ionesco:

Les personnages de Ionesco basent leur conversation sur le trivial, le banal, l'évident. Dans quelle mesure faisons-nous la même chose dans nos conversations quotidiennes? Pourquoi?

[Ionesco's characters base their conversations on the trivial, the obvious. Do we do the same thing in our daily conversations? Why?]

Role plays

Role plays add another dimension to personalization. Since illustrations speak louder than explanations, here again let us look at some examples, taken from *Ensuite* and *Moments Littéraires*.

1. Role play based on *Maria Chapdelaine* by Louis Hémon.

Maria is faced with a difficult choice: marrying one suitor, moving with him to Boston and benefiting from the ease and conveniences of city life, or marrying the farmer next door and continuing her difficult existence in the Canadian wilderness near her family. (*Ensuite*, p. 478)

Student A: You were born and raised in a small farming community, and you are thinking about moving to a big city. In one sense, you want to go, but you also want to stay. Express your feelings and ask for advice. Respond to your partners' enticements with further questions and reservations.

Student B: You are the advocate of the big city. Do everything you can to entice Student A to leave.

Student C: You are the advocate of the rural community. Do everything you can to convince Student A to stay.

2. Role play based on "Prière d'un petit enfant négre" by Guy Tirolien.

Student A: You are the teacher of the little child who hates to come to school. Find out why the boy feels the way he does, and try to convince his parent that school is important for him. Discuss the value of books, progress, and "civilization." Be persuasive.

Student B: You are the parent of the child, and you are torn between the old and the new ways. Defend your child and his desire to follow tradition. At the same time, ask more questions about what your child will learn in a Western school. Express your fears about the influence of Western civilization, based on what you have seen. Be open, yet skeptical.

3. Role play from "SYNTHESE" on the 16th century.

Imaginez une conversation à une terrasse de café entre les cinq auteurs de ce chapitre. Labé parle de ses souffrances en amour; Du Bellay décrit sa nostalgie de son pays natal. Les trois autres (Rabelais, Ronsard, Montaigne) vont essayer de les consoler. Basez vos paroles sur les idées et les sentiments exprimés dans les passages que vous avez lus.

[Imagine a conversation at a sidewalk cafe among the five authors in this chapter. Labé speaks of her love troubles; Du Bellay speaks of his homesickness. The other three (Rabelais, Ronsard, Montaigne) try to comfort them. Base what you say on the ideas and feelings expressed in the texts you have read.]

Games

The following games, all taken from Collie and Slater, also engage students personally.

Team competitions are an enjoyable way of reminding students about various aspects of a book or text. This can be done by straight-forward questions, or by using quotes: Who said this? Where? When? The questions can be prepared by the teacher or, better yet, by students in groups. The combing of the book or text to find suitable questions or quotes is in itself a useful revision exercise.

Retelling a story seems a fairly unsophisticated way of going over a book or text just read, yet there is no doubt that it can provide valuable oral practice in the foreign language. Much of the vocabulary needed will be known, and using it can help make it part of the learners' active lexis, while the narrative mode will usually allow them to use a variety of tenses, connecting words and other discourse markers.

For small classes, each student is given a number, then all the numbers are put into a hat. The student whose number is drawn first starts off, relating the story from the beginning, until interrupted by the teacher's buzzer. Another number is drawn and that student continues the narration. This can sometimes generate animated discussions about points omitted or related out of sequence.

A "**press conference**" is a good way to get students to put themselves back into a literary work they have just read. The roles are the following:

1. A press conference officer, who conducts the conference, calls on reporters to speak, keeps order, and brings the proceeding to a close.
2. One, two, or three characters from the book (as appropriate) are questioned by reporters and give their version of the events.
3. The rest of the class can be reporters. They can be given instructions on role cards ("Your editor would like you to find out. . .") to make sure that different angles of the story are investigated and to ensure a more lively press conference. The lower the level of the students, the more guidance questions they will need.

The debate is another popular game, where the class imagines that all major characters from the book or story they have just read are sailing high in a hot-air balloon, when they start to lose altitude. To prevent a crash, all but two of the characters must be thrown overboard. Each character has an opportunity to make a speech outlining the reasons why he or she should be allowed to remain in the balloon and survive. The teacher, or a student, presides. After the first round of speeches, the class votes for the two most convincing characters. The two survivors make a speech, summing up the crucial reasons, and trying to add new ones, for their continued survival. Finally, the class votes for the last remaining survivor.

This activity provides students with a common base of vocabulary and shared knowledge which facilitates the exercise. Students often comment with surprise on the insight they have suddenly gained into their character's psychology, because they have been forced to imaginatively put themselves into his or her place.

LITERATURE AS A SPRINGBOARD FOR WRITING ACTIVITIES

Connectors

The transition from sentence-level speech to paragraph-level speech is crucial at the intermediate level—that is, if we hope to help our students become Advanced speakers and writers. To make this transition, students need to work with connecting words, or the various ways to express relationships between ideas in the target language.

Literature is a perfect model and springboard for this, and writing is the best mode to start moving from sentences to paragraphs. The following activities can be used to work on connectors.

First, students learn to manipulate common connecting words in the target language, such as "first of all, then, finally, similarly, especially, actually, in other words, on the other hand, consequently," etc. Students can be asked to transform telegraphic-style sentences into a paragraph by adding the proper connectors. (Example taken from *Ensuite*, p. 342)

> Perspective du récit, dans l'ordre *chronologique*:
> Le renard se promène dans un bois / Il sent quelque chose de bon / Il lève la tête / Il voit un corbeau perché sur un arbre / Ce corbeau tient un fromage dans son bec / Le renard pense à une ruse / Il demande au corbeau si sa voix est aussi belle que son plumage / Le corbeau, flatté, commence à chanter / Quand il ouvre son bec, il perd son fromage / Le renard le prend / Le renard fait la morale au corbeau.

Students can also be asked to change a poem into prose or a narration rich in connecting words and original elaborations. "Déjeuner du matin," a well-known poem by Jacques Prévert, lends itself very well to this type of activity. Here is a second-year student's unaltered interpretation of "Déjeuner du matin."

> "*Déjeuner du matin*, c'est l'histoire d'un homme et sa femme quand ils prennent le petit déjeuner. C'est la femme qui raconte l'histoire, alors c'est son point de vue. Puisque la veille elle a conduite la voiture neuve de son mari et elle est rentrée dans un arbre, il est encore très fâché. Par conséquent il ne veut pas parler à elle, même qu'elle est assise près de lui. D'abord il met du café et du lait dans la tasse, et après ça du sucre. Mais il fait tout ça sans même la regarder. Elle sait qu'il est vraiment fâché, c'est-à-dire qu'il pense d'abord à son argent qui s'est perdu à cause de l'accident, mais surtout à la prestige qui s'est perdu avec sa précieuse BMW. Bien qu'elle veuille lui demander pardon, elle ne peut pas le faire puisqu'il ne lui parle pas ne la regarde. Finalement, il met son imperméable et part sous la pluie. Au moins il y a un arrêt d'autobus près de la maison. Après son départ elle commence à pleurer parce que, en fait, elle n'a pas d'assurance."
>
> [*Déjeuner du matin* is the story of a man and his wife as they are having breakfast. It is the woman who tells the story, so it is her point of view. Since the day before she drove her husband's new car into a tree, he is still mad at her. Therefore, he doesn't want to talk to her, even though

she is sitting next to him. First, he puts some coffee and milk in his cup, and after that some sugar. But he does this without looking at her. She knows that he is really mad, that is to say that he's thinking about the money that was lost because of the accident, but most of all about the prestige that was lost along with his precious BMW. Even though she wants to beg his forgiveness, she cannot do it because he won't look at her or talk to her. Finally, he puts on his raincoat and leaves in the rain. At least there is a bus stop close to the house. After his departure, she starts to cry because, actually, she doesn't have insurance.]

This work on connectors can be done as a follow-up to any reading assignment; students can be asked, in pairs, to write a 50-word summary of the reading passage, using a list of connectors written on the board by the teacher. Then there is comparison and discussion of the results.

Summarizing the summary

Students are divided into three groups. Each writes a summary of the section read, with a maximum number of words. They then pass on their summary to the next group, which must reduce it to half the number of words. This is now passed on to the third group, which halves the length again. Thus, each group is involved in reducing all three summaries. Final versions are read aloud and changes discussed.

This is a very useful cognitive activity. It teaches students how to separate the essential from the less important, focus on main ideas, and formulate thesis statements. As students become aware of ways of reducing, expanding, and connecting ideas, they are, indeed, being prepared to write better essays.

Awareness of various writing styles and registers

This is another preparation for good writing. Again, literature is the model and the springboard. In *Moments Littéraires*, students read a couple of letters by 17th century writer Mme de Sévigné. In the first letter, Mme de Sévigné writes to her daughter, inquiring about her trip from Paris to Lyon; the style is very formal, very "classique." As a follow-up, students are asked to imitate this style and work with constraints.

"Le style de Mme de Sévigné reflète les contraintes et conventions de la littérature du 17ᵉ siècle. A vous de faire une petite expérience avec des contraintes de style! Ecrivez sur un ton formel un paragraphe d'une "lettre" où Mme de Grignan décrit son voyage à sa mère. Défense absolue d'utiliser le verbe 'être'!"

[Mme de Sévigné's style reflects the constraints and conventions of 17th century literature. It is now your turn to experiment with style constraints! Write, in a formal tone, a paragraph from a letter where Mme de Grignan describes her trip to her mother. You are not allowed to use the verb "to be."]

In the second letter, Mme de Sévigné announces, with much suspense, some shocking news (the marriage of two famous people at the Court). The letter is full of stalling devices and superlatives ("La chose la plus étonnante, la plus merveilleuse, la plus miraculeuse, la plus triomphante, la plus singulière, la plus incroyable, la plus imprévue, la plus secrète, la plus brillante, etc.").

This writing activity follows.

"Pensez à un événement de l'actualité puis écrivez un paragraphe pour informer un(e) ami(e) de cet événement. Au lieu d'annoncer immédiatement la nouvelle, essayez d'augmenter sa curiosité par votre manière d'écrire. Vous pouvez imiter le style de Sévigné, avec beaucoup de superlatifs, ou vous pouvez utiliser une autre technique. Soyez prêt(e) à lire votre paragraphe à la classe."

[Think of a news event, then write a paragraph to inform a friend of this event. Instead of announcing the news right away, try to arouse his/her curiosity through your writing style. You may imitate Sévigné's style, with a lot of superlatives, or you may use another technique. Be prepared to read your paragraph to the class.]

Letters

Another popular activity is letter writing. Students are asked to write a letter that one of the main characters sends after the end of the book to explain what happened, and why.

After reading the novel *Pierre et Jean*, by Maupassant, students in a second-year course on introduction to literature were asked to write a letter that Pierre might have sent to his mother. The insight that students gained from this activity was profound. They were so involved with the book and their ideas that they forgot they were second-year students—and they wrote accordingly.

Literature has a way of engaging students so totally that linguistic obstacles are easier to overcome, especially if students are also given the strategies to deal with the linguistic tasks at hand. Some of the writing strategies needed in the proficiency-oriented classroom are the following:

—Avoid direct translation ("Do not translate, reformulate!")
—Generate ideas
—Keep the reader in mind
—Organize ideas
—Develop ideas
—Write introductions and conclusions
—Re-write: edit for content, proofread for form

It is easy to see that literature is a springboard for a wealth of language activities, but trying to do too many activities can harm the simple, personal involvement that students develop with the literary piece. The key is balance—activities that are varied, that complement each other and form a suitable balance between language-enrichment tasks and a deepening of students' understanding of the text. The principal aim of the whole operation is to foster enjoyment of reading in the learner. The best tasks, both in pre-reading and post-reading, are the ones that enhance this enjoyment, this personal involvement that makes literature so appealing in the language classroom.

CONCLUSIONS

"The ACTFL proficiency guidelines for language have radically transformed both methods and materials for teaching languages . . . the teaching of literature could stand a similar catalyst." (Rice, p. 14)

As the standards for cutting-edge foreign language classrooms have evolved since the 1979 President's Commission report, so should the place of literature in the foreign language curriculum. As instructors consider what they want students to be able to do with the foreign language before choosing what they should know, so may they look to what students will do with the literature they read, and to what the literature can help students do. From the beginning level on, the need may not be to simplify the text to be read, but to reconsider the tasks students are asked to perform. Literature and proficiency must cohabit the two-year college intermediate-level classroom of the 90's if we are to introduce the majority of foreign language students to the community of successful readers of literature. We should do no less.

BIBLIOGRAPHY

American Council on the Teaching of Foreign Languages. *ACTFL Proficiency Guidelines*. Hastings-on-Hudson: ACTFL, 1986.

Brumfit, C.J. and R.A. Carter. *Literature and Language Teaching*. New York: Oxford, 1986.

Collie, Joanne and Stephen Slater. *Literature in the Language Classroom*. New York: Cambridge, 1987.

Hirsch, Bette G. and Chantal P. Thompson. *Ensuite*. New York: McGraw-Hill, 1989.

Hirsch, Bette G. and Chantal P. Thompson. *Moments Littéraires*. Lexington: D.C. Heath, 1992.

Ionesco, Eugene. *La Cantatrice Chauve*. Paris: Gallimard, 1950.

Omaggio, Alice. *Teaching Language in Context: Proficiency-Oriented Instruction*. Boston: Heinle, 1986.

Rice, Donald. "Language Proficiency and Textual Theory: How the Twain Might Meet." *ADFL Bulletin*, 1991, Vol. 22, No. 1, pp. 12–15.

Part V

PARTICIPANTS: AACC FOREIGN LANGUAGE EDUCATION ROUNDTABLE

FEBRUARY 9–10, 1992   WASHINGTON, D.C.

DAVID A. BERRY
Executive Director
Community College Humanities
  Association;
Professor of History
Essex County College, NJ

FE PITTMAN BRITTAIN
Chair, Foreign Language
  Department
Pima Community College, AZ

MARY CASEY
Project Evaluator;
Professor of French
Prince George's Community
  College, MD

CARMEN CORACIDES
Chair, Foreign Language
  Department
Scottsdale Community College,
  AZ

DIANE U. EISENBERG
Project Co-director
AACC Foreign Language
  Education Project

ISA N. ENGLEBERG
Project Reporter
Prince George's Community
  College, MD

ROGER R. EKINS
Dean of Instruction
Butte College, CA

JAMES HERBERT
Director
NEH Division of Education

JUDY JEFFREY HOWARD
Program Officer
NEH Division of Education

BETTE G. HIRSCH
Division Chair, Foreign
  Language and
  Communications
Cabrillo College, CA

DORTHY JAMES
Professor of German
Hunter College, NY

EDWARD J. KIES
Dean of Humanities
College of DuPage, IL

RICHARD D. LAMBERT
Director
National Foreign Language
Center
Johns Hopkins University

JAMES F. McKENNEY
Director
AACC Office of Educational
Services

STEPHEN K. MITTELSTET
President
Richland College, TX

CONNIE ODEMS
Senior Vice President
AACC Professional Services

DAVID R. PIERCE
Project Co-director;
President, AACC

BEVERLY SIMONE
President
Madison Area Technical College,
WI;
Chair, AACC Board of Directors

JOYCE S. TSUNODA
Chancellor
University of Hawaii Community
College System

JOHN UNDERWOOD
Associate Professor
Spanish/Linguistics
Western Washington University

ELIZABETH WELLES
Program Officer
NEH Division of Education

"Language lies at the heart of the humanities. Foreign language instruction, when it includes serious study of culture, especially major works in history, literature, philosophy and the arts, is a vital part of a student's education in the humanities."

> David A. Berry
> Executive Director
> Community College Humanities Association;
> Professor of History
> Essex County College, NJ

"To learn a foreign language is to become aware of how a human being can function and communicate effectively in a manner different from oneself. This, indeed, enhances an acceptance and an understanding of diversity."

> Edward J. Kies
> Dean of Humanities
> College of DuPage, IL

"Living together harmoniously in today's world community requires cross-cultural understanding and language diversity. For many students the community college may provide the only opportunity to develop other languages and cultural understanding. We must not only provide the opportunity for our students, but extend a positive influence into elementary, secondary and university levels through articulation and cooperative language programs."

> Fe Brittain
> Chair, Foreign Language Department
> Pima Community College, AZ

"As the world gets smaller (and more difficult), it becomes critical that we encourage all our students to take a closer look at other cultures through learning languages. The community colleges will play a key role in the continuity of this process."

> John Underwood
> Associate Professor, Spanish/Linguistics
> Western Washington University

"If a student were to learn nothing more in a foreign language class than that he or she lived amidst a culture, the value of that experience would be assured."

> Bette G. Hirsch
> Division Chair, Foreign Language and Communications
> Cabrillo College, CA

"The necessary linking of foreign language instruction with general education should not be interpreted as adding yet another offering to a smorgasbord of courses in a rigid distribution arrangement. The AACC's Future Commission's Report calls for "a core curriculum . . . ~that_ focuses first on language, including the written and spoken symbol systems." Students need help to make connection across the disciplines and the study of languages can serve as one of the connecting bridges!"

> Joyce S. Tsunoda
> Chancellor
> University of Hawaii Community College System

"I strongly support the policy statement in all its aspects. The community college curriculum, if coordinated with the high school and the college curriculum, could play a crucial role in giving American students the six to eight years of sequenced instruction in a single foreign language long enjoyed in the European educational system, and essential to the widespread development of high levels of foreign language literacy. Serious attention will need to be paid to the practical issues referred to in Recommendation 5. Inner city community colleges, in particular, will need help in reducing their over-sized classes if foreign languages are to be seriously taught there."

> Dorothy James
> Professor of German
> Hunter College, NY